Home Style Cooking

Recipes From My Family & Friends To Yours

Liz Chartier

Avery Color Studios, Inc.
Gwinn, Michigan

© 2010 Avery Color Studios, Inc.

ISBN: 978-1-892384-54-6

Library of Congress Control Number: 2010901645

First Edition–2010

10   9   8   7   6   5   4   3   2   1

Published by Avery Color Studios, Inc.
Gwinn, Michigan 49841

Back cover photos: Author's Collection

This is for all of you, family and friends who have given me recipes and memories and have tried mine. And to the memory of the love of my life–to you, Pat.

Acknowledgements

I have fondly referred to this cookbook as "the third and final edition." Hopefully, this time I've gotten it right, because this is the last, the caboose, finis... I think...

Once again, so many have helped me with this endeavor. Several recipes were given to me by "Gug" the name fondly given to my mom by her grandchildren. New recipes from family near and far, and so many friends, great computer helpers, cousins Gunnar Flygh, Kristin Granli and friend Zenita Byers who helped with the Scandinavian section, sisters and daughters who helped organize and type, type, type. And a granddaughter who helped put it all together. A special thanks to my dear friend Judy McDonough. Thank you all. I'm forever in your debt.

My Grandma Kathinka "Gunga" Hansen

My Mother Janet "Gug" Orr

My Grandma Hazel "Bum Bum" Drevdahl

The recipes printed here have not been tested in laboratories, but their success has been established by friends, relatives and the most critical group of all – HUSBANDS AND FAMILY!!!

A Prayer For Each Day

Lord, we ask you to bless this family with a warm place by the fire when the world is cold; a light in the window when the way is dark; a welcoming smile when the road is long and a haven of love when the day is done. For the blessings of this home and this food, we give thanks.

Table Of Contents

Appetizers &
Beverages

Layered Taco Dip

12 ounces cream cheese
1-1/2 cups refried beans
1 bottle taco sauce, divided
3 tomatoes, chopped
1/2 green pepper, chopped
1/2 onion, chopped
shredded cheese

Spread cream cheese on a plate. Top with refried beans, taco sauce, tomato, green pepper, onion and the rest of the taco sauce. Top with shredded cheese and more taco sauce may be used if desired.

Elegant Liver Pate

3/4 cup butter
1 pound chicken livers
1 small onion, chopped
3/4 cup cooking wine
1/4 teaspoon ground mace
1/8 teaspoon pepper
1/2 cup croutons or 2 slices of toast

Heat 1/2 cup butter, add livers. When cooked, remove livers and sauté onions. Remove onions and add wine. Heat and stir, then put in blender. Add livers, seasonings, and onions, blend until smooth. Add remaining softened butter. Blend and put into bowl lined with saran wrap. Chill at least 3 hours. When ready to use, invert ball onto plate and frost with sour cream. Good served with crackers or small toasts.

Seasoned Oyster Crackers

1 package Hidden Valley Ranch® buttermilk dressing mix
1/4 teaspoon lemon pepper
1/2 - 1 teaspoon dill weed
1/4 teaspoon garlic powder
3/4 - 1 cup salad oil
12-16 ounces plain oyster crackers

Mix the first five ingredients well. Pour over crackers, stir to coat. Place on a cookie sheet in a warm oven for 15 to 20 minutes.

Ranch Pretzels

Sandy Boyd gave me this recipe and it is really good.

2 bags pretzels
1 package dry ranch dressing
1 tablespoon dill
1/2 teaspoon garlic powder
1/2 teaspoon onion salt
3/4 - 1 bottle Orville Redenbacher® butter flavored oil

Mix together first five ingredients and add flavored oil, stir to combine. Note: Some pretzels absorb better than others. It seems that those that have a shinier coating don't absorb as well. In that case use less oil.

Lollipops

green onions
cream cheese
milk
skinny ham

Cut some of the greens off the onions. Soften the cream cheese with some milk, spread liberally on onion, and wrap with ham. MMMMMM good!

Scrabble

1 stick margarine
1 tablespoon season salt
1/2 cup Worcestershire sauce
1 large box Crispix®
1 bag pretzel sticks
1 bag peanuts
Anything else your little heart desires

Melt margarine, add season salt and Worcestershire sauce, stirring until salt is dissolved. Combine the last three ingredients, pour margarine mixture on top and toss. Bake in roaster about an hour at 325°, stirring every 15 minutes. If you can find Chex® seasoning mix, it really works better.

Easy Cheese Fondue

1 can cheddar cheese soup
1 8-ounce package cream cheese
dash of Worcestershire sauce

Mix and keep warm, use as dip for French bread cubes which have been crisped in a frying pan with garlic butter.

Soyed Chicken Wings

3 pounds chicken wings
1/2 teaspoon ground ginger
1 teaspoon dry mustard
2 tablespoons oil
6 tablespoons soy sauce
Juice of 1 lemon

Marinate chicken wings with rest of ingredients in a plastic bag. Refrigerate for 1 hour or more. Place in pan, bake at 425° turning once, for 35 minutes or until done.

Seafood Canapés

1 or 2 cans chopped shrimp, crab, or lobster, drained
green onions to taste, chopped
2 cups cheese, shredded
squirt of lemon juice
dash of Worcestershire sauce
pastry shells

Combine first five ingredients well and press into small pastry shells (cream cheese pastry). Bake at 350° for 10 to 15 minutes.

Stuffed Raw Mushrooms

1 dozen medium mushrooms
6 - 8 ounces cream cheese, softened
1 teaspoon Worcestershire sauce
2 tablespoons minced onion or chives

Early in day, wash mushrooms, remove stems. Mix other ingredients, refrigerate. To serve, fill mushroom caps with cheese mixture.

Party Rye Treats

1/2 cup parmesan cheese
onion to taste, grated
1/2 cup mayo
party rye bread

Mix first 3 ingredients together and spread on party rye. Place on cookie sheet, under broiler, for a minute or two until bubbly and turns golden brown.

Cocktail Franks

1 large jar grape jelly
1 small jar mustard
squirt of lemon juice
2 pounds hot dogs, cut into 1 inch pieces or mini dogs

Heat first 3 ingredients, add hot dogs, serve hot. I always add a little horseradish, cranberry juice, and maybe some brandy or wine.

Cucumber Sandwiches

1 8-ounce package cream cheese
1/2 cup mayo
1/2 package dry Italian dressing mix
1 loaf party rye, sliced
cucumber slices
dill weed

Mix cream cheese, mayo and dressing. Spread on rye bread, add a slice of cucumber, and top with a dash of dill weed.

Dill Dip

1 pint sour cream
4 ounces cream cheese
2 teaspoons dill weed
2 tablespoons mayo
3 teaspoons dry onions
3 teaspoons parsley
seasoning salt to taste

Mix together, chill and serve. Great with veggies.

Deviled Ham Puffs

1 8-ounce package cream cheese
1 teaspoon grated onion
1/2 teaspoon baking powder
1 egg yolk
salt and pepper to taste
2 2-1/2 ounce cans deviled ham
18 small bread rounds

Mix cream cheese until soft, add all other ingredients except ham and bread. Spread each bread round with ham and top with a heaping teaspoon of the cheese mixture. Place on sheet pan in oven at 375° until slightly browned and puffy. About 8-10 minutes.

Some people are making such thorough preparations for rainy days, that they aren't enjoying today's sunshine!

Sombrero Dip

2 pounds ground beef
1 onion, chopped
1 can refried beans
about 1/4 cup ketchup, optional
green olives w/pimento
cheddar cheese, shredded
tortilla chips

Brown beef and some of the onion. Add beans and combine well. At this point I always add about a quarter cup of ketchup. Spread remaining onions, olives and cheese over meat mixture. Cover long enough for the cheese to melt. This stuff is to die for! Serve with tortilla chips.

Gug's Chip Dip

1 8-ounce package cream cheese
2 rounded tablespoons mayo or Miracle Whip®
2 teaspoons grated onion
2 tablespoons milk
1 teaspoon ketchup
1/4 teaspoon lemon juice
2 teaspoons Worcestershire sauce

Mix together and serve with chips or veggies. We grew up on this wonderful stuff.

Corned Beef Crisps

1 can corned beef, broken up well
minced onion to taste
just enough mayonnaise to hold mixture together
2 dozen bread rounds
Swiss cheese, shredded (If you like lots, use lots. It's melty and great!)

Combine corn beef, onion and mayo. Crisp up bread rounds in the oven. Top with corned beef mixture and top that with Swiss cheese. Put under the broiler until the cheese melts. Watch carefully, so the cheese doesn't burn. These are wonderful.

Senate Cheese Straws
This is another one of Gug's favorites.

1 pound sharp cheese
1-3/4 cups flour
1 teaspoon salt
1/4 - 1/2 teaspoon cayenne pepper
1/4 pound butter or margarine

Grate cheese, combine with other ingredients and beat until creamy, a food processor works great! Add a few drops of water if necessary to form firm dough. Divide in half and roll each section 1/4 inch thick. Cut into 6 x 3/8 inch strips, twist. Place on ungreased cookie sheet. Chill in freezer 15 minutes or longer to maintain shape. Bake at 350° for 10-12 minutes. Makes 5-6 dozen. I use a cookie press, it works great!

Yorkshire Devils

3 - 4 teaspoons oil
1 14-ounce can deviled ham
2 tablespoons bread crumbs
1/8 teaspoon ground sage
1 teaspoon green onions, minced

Batter:
1/2 cup flour
1 egg
1 cup milk
1/4 teaspoon salt

Put 1/8 - 1/4 teaspoon oil in each mini muffin tin. Combine ham, bread crumbs, sage and green onions. Roll into balls and put one in each muffin tin. Bake at 425° for 2 minutes. Combine batter ingredients and pour batter over meat. Bake at 425° until brown and puffed, 25 minutes.

Vegetable Pizza

2 packages crescent rolls
12 ounces cream cheese
1 package Good Seasonings® salad dressing mix
1/2 cup salad dressing
celery, onion, green peppers, tomatoes, mushrooms, green and black olives
shredded cheese

Pat crescents in cookie sheet, bake at 350° for 10 minutes. Cool for 10 minutes. Mix cream cheese, dressing mix and salad dressing, spread on top. Top with remaining ingredients and serve.

*A very nice variation of this is a holiday tree. To do this, just cut 1 package of crescent rolls into 16 slices. Lay together on a cookie sheet, to form a tree. 5 slices for the bottom of the tree, and going up to 1 for the top. Use 1 slice for the trunk. then finish the same as a regular veggie pizza, using more red and green toppings.

Cocktail Meatballs

1 can jellied cranberries
1 jar chili sauce
2 tablespoons brown sugar
2 tablespoons lemon juice
meatballs

Combine the cranberries, chili sauce, brown sugar and lemon juice. Make a batch of your favorite meatballs and simmer in this sauce.

Shrimp And Mushroom Puffs

2 8-ounce packages cream cheese
3 egg yolks
1/2 cup mayonnaise
1/2 cup parmesan cheese
2 tablespoons grated onion
garlic salt to taste
1/2 green pepper
1 can deviled shrimp, rinsed
1 can sliced mushrooms, drained
English muffins

Cream first 6 ingredients. Chop green pepper, shrimp and mushrooms and add to creamed mixture. Split muffins, spread each half with 1 scant 1/4 cup of cheese mixture. Cut into quarters and place on cookie sheet. Broil until golden brown. Watch, they burn fast! Serve.

Quick And Easy Tex Mex Dip

8 ounces cream cheese
1 can of chili, without beans
1 - 2 cups mozzarella cheese, shredded

Spread cream cheese on the bottom of a 10 inch pie plate. Top with chili. Spread mozzarella cheese on top. Bake in a 350° oven until the cheese melts. This is really yummy.

Spinach Dip

1 10-ounce package chopped spinach
1-1/2 cups sour cream
1 cup mayonnaise
1 package Knorr® vegetable soup mix
1 8-ounce can water chestnuts, drained
3 green onions, chopped

Thaw and squeeze chopped spinach until dry. Stir together spinach, sour cream, mayonnaise, soup mix, chestnuts and chopped onions, blend well. Cover, refrigerate 2 hours. Stir before serving.

Deviled Eggs

6 hard cooked eggs
1 teaspoon mustard
1/4 teaspoon salt
1/8 teaspoon pepper
2 tablespoons mayonnaise
dash of Worcestershire sauce

Shell eggs, cut each in half and remove yolks. Mash the yolks and add rest of ingredients. Mix until smooth. Fill whites of eggs with mixture, dust with paprika, chill.

Mexican Appetizer Dish

2 pounds hamburger
1 package taco seasoning
2 8-ounce packages cream cheese
1 16-ounce sour cream
6 green onions, chopped

Brown hamburger, add seasoning. Spread into 9 x 13 inch pan. Mix all other ingredients together and spread over meat. Bake at 350° for 20 minutes.

Appetizers & Beverages

Puppy Chow

1 cup chocolate chips
1 cup peanut butter
1 stick margarine
6 cups Crispix® cereal
2 cups powdered sugar

Melt together chips, peanut butter and margarine, until smooth. Pour over cereal and mix well. Put half the mixture into a grocery bag, add 1 cup powdered sugar and shake well to coat. Pour into a bowl. Repeat with other half of cereal and cup of powdered sugar. Serve.

Spiced Praline Pecans

1/4 cup maple syrup
1/2 cup brown sugar (light or dark)
1/4 teaspoon cinnamon
2 cups pecan halves (or any nuts you choose)

Mix all ingredients except pecans. Then toss with the nuts to evenly coat. Spread on a greased cookie sheet and bake at 250° for an hour. Stir every 15 minutes. These will keep in an airtight container for a few weeks.

Hot Dip

2 pounds Velveeta® cheese, melted
1 quart tomatoes, no juice
1 cup onions, chopped
1 can chopped jalapeno peppers with tomatoes or jalapeno relish (hotter!)
2 small cans chopped green chilies

Mix all together. Keep and serve warm with tortilla chips. For a quicker version, use canned Rotel with the Velveeta®.

Cheese Broccoli Squares

3 tablespoons butter
2 10-ounce packages chopped frozen broccoli
3 large eggs
1 cup milk
1 cup flour
1 teaspoon baking powder
salt
2 tablespoons onion, chopped
1 pound cheddar cheese, shredded

Grease a 9 x 13 inch pan with butter. Steam broccoli until done. Cool and press dry. Beat eggs until frothy, add milk. Add flour, baking powder and salt. Fold in broccoli, onions and cheese. Put in pan, sprinkle lightly with seasoned salt. Bake at 350° for 35 minutes. This is a favorite!

Red Pepper Jelly

3/4 cup red bell peppers
1/4 cup hot red peppers
6-1/2 cups sugar
1-1/2 cups apple cider vinegar
1 bottle or 2 pouches of Certo®

Grind and retain juice from peppers. Combine with sugar and vinegar. Bring to a boil for 10 minutes. Remove from heat and add Certo®. Stir for 5 minutes. You can add a little red food color it you like. Pour into small jars and seal with wax. Pour over a block of cream cheese and serve cold with crackers for a good appetizer. DO NOT USE BLENDER OR PROCESSOR! I have added raspberries to this recipe in place of bell peppers. It's great.

Chicken And Bacon Roll Ups

1 pound bacon
about 1-1/2 pounds boneless, skinless, chicken breasts
2/3 cup brown sugar
2 tablespoons chili powder

Cut bacon slices into thirds. Cut chicken into 1-1/2 inch chunks. Wrap the chicken with bacon strips and fasten with a toothpick. Mix the sugar and chili powder. Roll the chicken bundles in the sugar mixture and place them on a rack on a baking sheet. Bake at 350° for 25-30 minutes or until bacon is crispy.

The Lord sometimes takes us into troubled waters.
Not to drown us, but to cleanse us.

Rumaki

1 carton chicken livers
1/2 cup dry vermouth, divided
water chestnuts, halved
bacon, sliced thin
1 clove of garlic, thinly sliced
1/2 cup soy sauce
1 slice of ginger or 1 teaspoon ground ginger
minced onion

Saute chicken livers in 1/4 cup dry vermouth. Cut livers in half and sandwich between 2 water chestnut halves. Wrap with a thin slice of bacon and fasten with a toothpick. Marinate in a mixture of the remaining 1/4 cup vermouth, garlic, soy sauce, ginger and onion for several hours, turning occasionally. Drain and broil until bacon is crisp. I often put the bacon slices in the oven for a few minutes before I wrap the rumaki. It seems to cut down on splattering during broiling. This is great!

Crab Wontons

Molly came up with this and it's great. Don't eat too many…

1 8-ounce package cream cheese
1 pouch of crab meat
4 green onions, chopped
2 capsful of soy sauce
wonton skins

Mix the first 4 ingredients to make the filling. Lay out the wonton skins. Place a good rounded teaspoon of the filling in the center. Moisten the edges, and bring them to the center, pressing together so that the filling doesn't leak. Deep fry just until they begin to turn golden brown, about 10-15 seconds. Put on towels to drain and serve with sweet and sour sauce. This filling is actually better made the day before.

Onion Rings

1 large sweet onion
1 cup flour
2 teaspoons salt
1-1/2 tsp. baking powder
1 egg yolk
2/3 cup milk
1 tablespoon oil
1 egg white

Slice onion and soak rings in cold water for 30 minutes. Drain and pat dry with paper towels. Mix flour, salt and baking powder well and set aside. Mix egg yolk, milk and oil until well blended and pour into flour mixture. Mix well until thick and creamy. Beat egg white until stiff and add to the rest of the batter. Dip onion rings into batter allowing excess batter to drip back into bowl. Fry in hot oil until golden.

Bacon, Cheese And Almond Spread

This is great stuff!

1/3 cup almonds, slivered and toasted in the oven
3 - 4 slices crisp bacon, crumbled
1/2 cup cheddar cheese, shredded
3/4 cup mayonnaise or salad dressing
1/3 cup minced onion
salt to taste

Mix all ingredients together and serve. When doubling recipe, use only 1 cup mayonnaise.

Pimento And Cheese Spread

1 8-ounce package cream cheese
1 cup real mayonnaise
2 teaspoons onion, grated
3/4 teaspoon salt
1/8 teaspoon pepper
1/8 teaspoon granulated garlic
2 cups cheddar cheese, shredded
2 cups monterey jack cheese, shredded (or 4 cups shredded cheese blend)
1 4-ounce jar diced pimento

Mix the cream cheese, mayonnaise, onion and spices well. Add the cheese and pimento. Refrigerate. It's great for sandwiches or just for crackers.

Quick Shrimp Or Crab Appetizers

1 8-ounce package cream cheese
seafood sauce
shrimp or crab

Put block of cream cheese on plate and top with seafood sauce and sprinkle shrimp or crab on top. Serve with Triscuits®. You can also spread cream cheese on a plate and top in the same way.

Cheese Canapés

8 ounces sharp cheddar cheese, shredded
6 tablespoons margarine
6 tablespoons mayonnaise
1 egg, well beaten
1 teaspoon minced onion
party rye bread, sliced

Mash softened cheese with fork. Add remaining ingredients, except the bread. Spread on slices of party rye bread. Put under broiler until bubbly and golden brown.

Cream Cheese Mold

2 8-ounce packages cream cheese
1/2 cup mayonnaise
1/3 cup parmesan cheese
1/2 cup chopped ham, crisp bacon or chipped beef
1/4 cup each green pepper and green onion, chopped

Mix cheese and mayonnaise with mixer. Fold in remaining ingredients with a spoon. Can be molded or served in a bowl. This is also a wonderful filling for cherry tomatoes.

Karen's Pico De Gallo

6 roma tomatoes, diced
1 large jalapeno pepper, seeded and minced
1 bunch (about 5) green onions, diced
1 large avocado, diced
2 - 3 cloves garlic, minced or grated
cilantro and kosher salt to taste
juice of 1 lime

Mix all these ingredients together. This is the best!

Salsa

This recipe came from Gigi MacGregor in Arizona and it is really great!

1 can mild, diced green chilies
2 cans chopped tomatoes
2 cloves garlic, pressed
1 medium onion, chopped
1/2 teaspoon cumin or coriander or 2 tablespoons cilantro

Mix and serve with tortilla chips.

Hot Swiss Cheese Dip

2 cups mayonnaise
2 cups swiss cheese, grated
1 - 2 cups frozen chopped onion
1/2 teaspoon dill weed
dab mustard

Combine ingredients in a small bowl and bake at 350° for 20 minutes. Serve warm with Triscuits®.

Green Onion Dip

Ginger Boyd brought this to a get together. It is so easy and good, but you must use a blender or processor.

3 green onions
1 8-ounce package cream cheese
1 8-ounce sour cream
a little garlic salt

Chop green onions in blender with a little water. Add remaining ingredients. Mix well and chill.

Spinach Artichoke Dip

3/4 - 1 cup butter
1 14-ounce jar water packed artichokes, drained and rough chopped
1 10-ounce package frozen chopped spinach, thawed and water squeezed out
1 8-ounce package cream cheese, softened
16 ounces sour cream
1 cup grated parmesan cheese
1 can water chestnuts, drained and roughly chopped
1 clove garlic, minced
chives to taste

Melt the butter. Stir in artichokes and spinach. Cook about 5 minutes. Add cream cheese and sour cream, then stir in remaining ingredients. This may be done on the stove top or in the oven at 350° for 20 minutes. Serve warm with crackers, large croutons or veggies.

Laughter is a tranquilizer with no side effects.

Asparagus Roll-ups
This is really delicious.

32 fresh thin asparagus spears
16 slices sandwich bread, crusts removed
1 package cream cheese (8-ounce), softened
8 strips crisp cooked bacon, crumbled
2 tablespoons chives, chopped
1/4 cup melted butter or margarine
3 tablespoons parmesan cheese

Blanch asparagus in a skillet with a small amount of water for about 2-4 minutes. Put into ice bath. Drain. Flatten bread with a rolling pin. Combine cream cheese, bacon and chives and spread 1-2 tablespoons on each slice. Top with 2 asparagus spears, placed in opposite directions and roll up tightly. Place seam side down on a greased cookie sheet. Brush with melted butter, and sprinkle with parmesan cheese. Cut each roll up in half diagonally. Bake at 400° for 10 minutes or until lightly brown. Makes 32.

Tortilla Roll-ups

1 8-ounce package cream cheese, creamed with a little milk
chopped olives, to taste
grated cheese, to taste
chilies, chopped, ti taste
1/2 cup mayonnaise
ham
4-6 flour tortillas

Mix all ingredients, except tortillas, spread on flour tortillas (any flavor). Roll tortilla and wrap in saran wrap. Chill, cut in bite size pieces, serve with salsa or plain.

Mini Ham Tarts

2 - 3 ounces ham, chopped
1/4 cup onion, chopped
1/2 cup swiss cheese, shredded
1 egg
1-1/2 teaspoons dijon mustard
1/8 teaspoon pepper
1 8-ounce package crescent rolls

Combine ham and onion. Add cheese, egg, mustard and pepper. Mix well. Lightly spray mini muffin pans. Unroll crescent rolls and press them into a rectangle. Cut into 24 pieces. Press into muffin tins and fill each one with ham mixture. Bake at 350° for 13-15 minutes or until golden brown. Makes 24 tarts.

Crab Dip

This is Clara Bosanic's recipe and it's a keeper!

1 8-ounce package cream cheese
1 package imitation crab, chopped
1 - 2 green onions, chopped
1/4 cup ranch dressing

Mix well and serve with crackers.

Crab Dip II

This came from my dear friend, Kathy Aldrich. For some reason, hers is always better than mine. Mmmmm.

1 8-ounce package cream cheese
1 teaspoon garlic powder
1 teaspoon onion powder
1/3 cup each celery and green onion, finely diced
4 - 6 ounces crab, diced or shredded
salt to taste

Mix all together and refrigerate.

Mini Creme Puffs

1/2 cup butter
1 cup water
1 cup flour
4 eggs

In saucepan, melt butter and add water. Bring to a boil and add the flour. Stir until it forms a ball. Transfer to mixer and add eggs one at a time. Drop from a teaspoon onto an ungreased cookie sheet, about 1 inch apart. Bake at 450° for 10 minutes, then reduce heat to 350° and bake for another 10 minutes or until golden brown. When cool, cut off top and fill with any sandwich mixture or for a dessert, fill with custard and drizzle with chocolate or caramel. This makes a wonderful appetizer.

Pinwheel Sandwiches

Order sandwich bread that is sliced across. Cut off the crusts. Flatten each slice with a rolling pin and spread each slice with a sandwich mixture, such as: egg salad, tuna salad, ham salad or chicken salad. Roll up each slice and wrap tightly in plastic wrap. Keep in refrigerator until used. These sandwiches also freeze well.

Smoked Whitefish Dip

1 8-ounce cream cheese
1 small container onion dip
1/2 tablespoon dried parsley
1 tablespoon chives, chopped
1 teaspoon granulated garlic
4-6 drops hot sauce
1 pound smoked whitefish, bones removed

Combine everything except the fish. Mix well and add boned fish. Refrigerate 6 hours or overnight. Serve with crackers

Cranberry Slush

1 quart cranberry juice
1 can frozen lemonade
1 lemonade can of brandy

Mix all together and freeze. When ready to serve, fill glasses half full of slush and add some 50-50.

Mofforr

Once upon a time, long, long ago (when the Pilgrims came over on the *Mayflower*), my parents, the Orrs, and their very best friends, the Moffats, invented this cocktail. I really think all of their descendants should have it. So here goes:

1/2 jigger bourbon
1/2 jigger brandy
1/2 teaspoon sugar
1/2 dash bitters
1part/squidge of orange and lemon juice

Shake like hell on ice and drink, drink, drink.

Punch

2 packages raspberry Kool-aid®
2 cups sugar
1 small can frozen orange juice
1 small can frozen lemonade
3-1/2 quarts water
1 large bottle of 7-Up®

Mix all except 7-Up®. Add 7-Up® just before serving.

Irish Cream

4 eggs
1 carton coffee rich
1 can sweetened condensed milk
1-1/2 cups blended whiskey (I use Jim Beam®)
1/2 teaspoon instant coffee
1/2 teaspoon coconut extract
1 teaspoon vanilla
1/8 teaspoon almond extract
1 tablespoon chocolate syrup

Beat eggs, coffee rich and milk with mixer, then add the rest. Transfer all to blender and blend for 2 minutes. Pour into bottle and store in refrigerator.

Kahlua

1-1/4 cups instant coffee
1 quart water
3 pounds sugar
1-1/2 quarts water
2 ounces vanilla
fifth of vodka

Boil together the instant coffee and water. Let cool. Boil together sugar and water. Let cool. When all is reasonably cool, combine them. Add vanilla and vodka. Pour into bottles.

Slush

> 1 large can frozen lemonade
> 1 large can frozen limeade
> 1 lemonade can of rum
> 2 lemonade cans of water

Mix all and freeze. Serve with 7-Up® or 50-50.

Peaches And Cream

> 1 can sweetened condensed milk
> 1 cup peach schnapps
> 1 cup heavy cream
> 3/4 cup vodka
> 4 eggs
> 1 teaspoon vanilla
> 1/4 teaspoon almond extract

Blend until smooth. Shake before using. Makes 2-1/2 pints.

Peachy Keen Slush

My sister, Jeffy makes this every Christmas. Very good.

> 1/4 cup sugar
> 2 cups water
> 1 12-ounce can frozen orange juice
> 1 12-ounce can frozen lemonade
> 3 cups water
> 2-1/2 cups Peach Schnapps
> 1/3 cup lemon juice

Boil sugar and 2 cups water for 3 minutes. Let cool. Combine sugar mixture and orange juice and lemonade in a glass or plastic container. Add 3 cups water, Schnapps and lemon juice. Cover and freeze. To serve, fill glass 3/4 full with slush and add ginger ale.

Salads & Dressings

Shrimp Salad

2-1/2 tablespoons chicken bouillon crystals
enough mayonnaise to hold together
1 14-ounce bag shell macaroni, cooked
2 cans small shrimp
1 - 2 tomatoes
1/2 teaspoon garlic powder
1 tablespoon Worcestershire sauce
1 medium onion, chopped
2 stalks celery, leaves included, diced
salt and pepper
pinch of parsley

Heat 1 shrimp can of water with bouillon. Mix with mayonnaise. Mix with all other ingredients. Chill. Optional additions: peas, cheese, hard boiled eggs, dill, a dash of horseradish.

Tuna Salad

The universal picnic salad!

small bag or box any pasta
1 - 2 cans good tuna
1 small onion, chopped
1 - 2 stalks celery, diced
1/2 cup peas
2 - 3 hard boiled eggs, chopped
olives, optional
potato salad dressing

Cook pasta, add tuna, onion, celery, peas, eggs, and olives if you like. Mix gently and dress with potato salad dressing, found on page 40.

The devil has many tools, but a lie is the handle that fits them all.

Really Good Chicken Salad

2 cups cooked chicken breast, diced
1 cup celery, finely diced
1/4 cup crushed pineapple, well drained
2 green onions, finely sliced
1 can sliced water chestnuts, drained and chopped
2 tablespoons diced pimento

Mix together and chill.

Combine 1/3 cup mayo or salad dressing
1 tablespoon soy sauce
1 teaspoon lemon juice

Mix with the chilled mixture. Served chilled. Great on endive leaves for an appetizer or as a lunch.

Cranberry Salad Mold

2 small packages cherry Jello®
3 cups boiling water
1 can whole cranberry sauce
1 cup celery, diced
1 can crushed pineapple, drained
1/2 - 1 cup walnuts, chopped
1 8-ounce container sour cream
1/4 cup salad dressing
milk to thin

Mix Jello® and water. Chill until starts to set, then add cramberry sauce, celery, pineapple and walnuts and mix well. Put in mold and let set several hours or overnight. Mix together sour cream and salad dressing, using milk to thin. Serve over jello mold.

Apricot And Cheese Delight Salad

3 3-ounce orange or orange pineapple Jello®
3 cups boiling water
1-1/2 cups apricot juice
1 medium or large can apricots, drained, chopped small, reserving juice
1 medium or large can crushed pineapple, drained, reserve juice
1-1/2 cups small marshmallows

Keep apricot and pineapple juice separate. Dissolve Jello® in boiling water, add apricot juice, fruits and marshmallows. Chill until firm.

Topping:
1/2 cup sugar
3 tablespoons flour
1 egg, beaten
2 tablespoons butter
1 cup pineapple juice or part apricot
1-1/2 cups Cool Whip®
3/4 cup cheddar cheese, shredded

Blend sugar and flour with egg. Add butter and juice. Cook over low heat, stirring until thick. Cool and fold in Cool Whip®. Spread over Jello® and top with cheese.

Baked Pineapple

Cream together:
1/2 cup sugar
1 cup margarine
2 eggs

Add:
1/2 cup milk
5 slices of bread, cubed
1 large can chunk pineapple with juice

Put into greased baking dish and bake for 1 hour at 350°. Serve warm.

Cherry Cranberry Salad

1-3/4 cups water
1/4 cup sugar
1 16-ounce can tart cherries or frozen cherries
1 can whole cranberries
1 6-ounce cherry Jello®
1 3-ounce lemon Jello®
1 cup boiling water
1 3-ounce cream cheese
1/3 cup salad dressing
1 8-1/4 ounce can undrained crushed pineapple (syrup pack)
1/2 pint whipping cream
1 cup mini marshmallows
2 tablespoons chopped nuts

Bring water and sugar to a boil. Stir in cherries, cover, reduce heat and simmer for 10 minutes. Add cranberries and cherry Jello®. Cook until dissolved and pour into a 9 x 13 inch pan. Chill. Dissolve lemon Jello® in water and beat cream cheese with salad dressing. Gradually add to Jello®. Stir in undrained pineapple. Chill until partly set. Whip whipping cream and fold into lemon Jello®. Fold in marshmallows. spread over cherry Jello® and sprinkle with chopped nuts. Chill until firm. Whew!!!!!

Red Raspberry Jello® Salad

Lisa makes this and says there's never any left. Good stuff...

2 3-ounce packages raspberry Jello®
2 cups hot water
2 10-ounce packages frozen raspberries, partially defrosted
1 20-ounce can crushed pineapple, drained
2 3-ounce cream cheese
12 large marshmallows (melted in microwave)
1 cup whipping cream
1/4 cup sugar

Dissolve raspberry Jello® in water. Add raspberries and pineapple and pour into 9 x 13 inch pan. Chill until set. Combine cream cheese and melted marshmallows. Whip the cream with sugar. Add the cream cheese mixture and top the Jello®. Chill again.

Orange Sherbet Salad

1 large package orange Jello®
2 cups boiling water
1 pint orange sherbet
2 cans mandarin oranges, drained, divided
1 small can crushed pineapple or tidbits, drained
handful mini marshmallows
a little coconut
enough sour cream to hold mixture together

Mix the Jello® with the boiling water, mix in the orange sherbet and 1 can mandarin oranges. Put in ring mold and set. Mix together the remaining can of oranges, the pineapple, marshmallows, coconut and sour cream. Unmold jello mixture and fill center with the sour cream mixture.

Real love is helping someone who can't return the favor.

Taffy Apple Salad

6 ounces pineapple juice
2 tablespoons vinegar
2 tablespoons flour
1 cup sugar
6 cups apple, chopped or sliced
1 cup peanuts
1 8-ounce Cool Whip®

In saucepan, combine juice, vinegar, flour and sugar. Cook until thick, stirring constantly. Remove from heat and cool. Mix with apples and nuts. Add Cool Whip® last, and refrigerate.

Grape Salad

1 8-ounce package cream cheese
1 8-ounce sour cream
1/2 cup sugar
1 teaspoon vanilla
3 pounds green and red grapes, (1-1/2 pounds of each)
1/2 cup brown sugar
1 tablespoon butter, melted
nuts, chopped, optional

Cream the cream cheese, sour cream, sugar and vanilla, fold in the grapes. Top with a mixture of the brown sugar and butter. Sprinkle with chopped nuts of your choice.

Jello® Fruit Fluff

1 can well drained fruit
1 package Jello® (flavor to compliment fruit)
1 pound cottage cheese
1 large Cool Whip®

Mix thoroughly, chill. Serve.

Pink Aztec Freeze Salad

2 3-ounce cream cheese
2 tablespoons mayonnaise
1 can whole cranberries
1 9-ounce can crushed pineapple, drained
1/2 cup nuts, chopped
1 cup whipping cream, whipped with 2 tablespoons powdered sugar

Cream together the cream cheese and mayonnaise, add the fruit and nuts. Fold in whipped cream and pour into a loaf pan or muffin tins and freeze overnight. Slice and serve on greens. Great for those do ahead meals.

Cucumber Salad Mold

I make this one for Julie's birthday. It's her favorite.

1 small onion
1 medium cucumber
1 pound cottage cheese
1/2 cup mayonnaise
salt to taste
1 3-ounce lime Jello®
1/2 cup hot water

Blend the onion and cucumber in a blender or food processor. Add the cottage cheese, mayonnaise and salt. Dissolve the jello in hot water and add to the mixture. Mix everything well and put into a bowl or mold. Keep in refrigerator until well set.

24 Hour Salad

1/4 cup cream
3 egg yolks, beaten well
juice of one lemon (1/2 if large)
pinch of salt
1 cup whipped cream
1 can pineapple chunks or tidbits, drained
1 can crushed pineapple, drained
1 can fruit cocktail, drained
1/2 pound mini marshmallows
seedless green grapes
1 cup almonds, chopped, optional

Cook the cream, egg yolks, lemon juice and salt to a smooth custard. Cool then add the whipped cream. This custard will "NOT" taste sweet, the fruit flavors it nicely. Add the pineapple, fruit cocktail, marshmallows, grapes and almonds. Let stand in refrigerator overnight.

Orange Cream Fruit Salad

1 20-ounce can pineapple chunks, drained
1 16-ounce can mandarin oranges
1 11-ounce can mandarin oranges
3 medium bananas, sliced
1 small package instant French vanilla pudding
1-1/2 cups milk
3-ounces frozen orange juice concentrate, thawed
3/4 cup sour cream

In large bowl, mix fruits and set aside. Mix together pudding, milk and orange juice. Add sour cream. Fold in fruit and chill at least 4 hours.

Sweet Sauerkraut Salad

Robbie Boyd brought this salad in to work and it was a real hit!

32-ounces sauerkraut, rinsed and drained
1 medium onion, chopped
1 red pepper, chopped
1 green pepper, chopped
4 stalks celery, diced
4 carrots, shredded
1 cup water chestnuts
2 tablespoons whole mustard seed
2 tablespoons caraway seed
1-1/3 cups sugar
2/3 cup vinegar

Combine the vegetables and spices. Dissolve sugar and vinegar over heat and pour over vegetables. Mix well and chill.

Broccoli Salad

1 bunch fresh broccoli, broken into small florets
1 small onion, chopped coarsely
1/2 pound bacon, cooked crisp, diced
1/4 cup sugar
2 tablespoons vinegar
1-1/2 cups salad dressing

Toss the broccoli, onion and bacon together. Combine the sugar, vinegar and salad dressing, mixing well. Pour over broccoli mixture, toss to combine.

A good variation to this salad is:

Cauliflower, Pea and Peanut Salad

1 head cauliflower, broken into florets
1-1/2 cups frozen peas
1-1/2 cups peanut

Use the same dressing as the broccoli salad above.

Three Bean Salad

1 can green beans, drained
1 can wax beans, drained
1 can kidney beans, drained and rinsed
1 small green pepper, chopped
2 cups celery, diced
1 onion, thinly sliced
1 teaspoon salt
1/2 cup sugar
1/2 cup salad oil
1/2 cup vinegar

Mix first 6 ingredients together. Mix salt, sugar, salad oil and vinegar, bring to a boil to dissolve sugar and cool. Pour over vegetables. Mix and refrigerate 24 hours.

Coleslaw

1 head of cabbage
carrot, shredded, optional
red cabbage, optional

Chop cabbage finely. If desired add shredded carrot and red cabbage for color. Dress with the coleslaw dressing below. For a little change, add some mini marshmallows and pineapple to this salad. It gives it a whole different complexion.

Coleslaw Dressing

This is Mom's.

1 teaspoon salt
1 cup sugar
1/2 teaspoon celery seed
1 teaspoon paprika
1 teaspoon onion juice or grated onion
1/2 cup vinegar
1/2 teaspoon dry mustard
1 cup oil

Mix well in blender. Blend for 10 minutes.

Marinated Brussels Sprouts

This is one of Mom's quick, good treats.

frozen brussels sprouts, thawed
onion, sliced
Italian dressing

Mix the brussels sprouts with onion slices, red onion is nice. Marinate in Italian dressing. They're different and very good.

Wilted Lettuce Or Spinach Salad

4 - 5 slices bacon, cut up
1 medium onion, sliced
1 tablespoon sugar
2 tablespoons vinegar
1/2 teaspoon salt
1/8 teaspoon pepper
1 large bunch leaf lettuce or spinach, torn into pieces

Fry bacon until crisp, drain most of the bacon grease, reserving 1 - 2 tablespoons. Cook onion in bacon grease until not quite tender. Remove from heat. Stir in remaining ingredients except greens. Heat just to boiling. Cool just slightly and pour over greens. Sprinkle bacon over salad.

As soon as the rush is over I'm going to have a nervous breakdown.
I worked for it, I owe it to myself and no one is going to deprive me of it!

7-Layer Salad

In glass cake pan (glass to show the layers) layer the following:
First layer: lettuce, chopped
Second layer: celery, diced
Third layer: green pepper, diced
Forth layer: onion, chopped
Fifth layer: frozen peas and 1 can sliced water chestnuts
Sixth layer: Miracle Whip® or ranch dressing, spread right to the edges of the pan
Seventh layer: shredded cheese
Top with crisp diced bacon. Refrigerate for an hour or so before serving.

Potato Salad

6 - 7 potatoes (not bakers), unpeeled and cooked until tender
1 medium onion, chopped finely
2 - 3 stalks celery, diced
3 - 4 hard boiled eggs, chopped (reserve 1 egg for garnish)
salt and pepper

Peel and cube cold potatoes, add the rest of ingredients, adding eggs last. Dress with potato salad dressing found below. Let set a few hours or even overnight before serving.

Potato Salad And Pasta Salad Dressing

2 cups salad dressing
1/2 cup sour cream, optional
thin with a little milk
Add: about 1 tablespoon each: mustard, sugar and vinegar

Mix well and dress salad.

Pasta Salad
This is Lisa's favorite to make.

1 pound spaghetti, rotini or pasta of your choice
tomatoes, chopped
onion, chopped
green & red peppers, chopped
1 small can sliced black olives
6 ounces pepperoni, ham or salami, diced
8 ounces fresh mozzarella, diced
1 bottle Zesty Italian dressing

Cook pasta according to package directions, drain and rinse with cold water. Combine the pasta with tomatoes, cucumbers and onion. Sprinkle with seasoning and dress with the Italian dressing.

German Potato Salad

6 - 8 potatoes (not bakers)
1 pound bacon, diced
1 onion, diced
1/2 cup water
3/4 cup sugar
2 tablespoons flour
2 tablespoons vinegar
hardboiled eggs, cut into quarters
chives, chopped
paprika

Boil potatoes in skins until done. Cool completely. Brown bacon until crisp. Drain fat, reserving 1 - 2 tablespoons. Add to bacon fat the onion and cook until onion is translucent. Add water, sugar mixed with the flour, and vinegar. Cook together until slightly thickened. Slice potatoes into flat casserole, and add dressing between layers of potatoes to insure equal coating. Pour any remaining dressing over the top. Garnish with eggs. Sprinkle with chives and paprika. Best served at room temperature.

Wonderful Blue Cheese Dressing

Mmmmm good! Cousin Karen sent me this and we use it on everything.

1/3 cup mayo
2/3 cup sour cream
1 tablespoon white wine vinegar
1/2 teaspoon garlic salt
1/8 teaspoon white pepper
1/8 teaspoon dry mustard
1/2 cup blue cheese, crumbled

Mix well and add blue cheese.

Coleslaw Dressing

This is Mom's.

1 teaspoon salt
1 cup sugar
1/2 teaspoon celery seed
1 teaspoon paprika
1 teaspoon onion juice or grated onion
1/2 cup vinegar
1/2 teaspoon dry mustard
1 cup oil

Mix well in blender. Blend for 10 minutes.

French Dressing

1/2 cup oil
1/2 cup sugar or honey
1/2 cup ketchup or chili sauce
1 teaspoon salt
Optional: grated onion, garlic, lemon

Mix well, this keeps very well.

Celery Seed Dressing

1-1/2 cups sugar
2/3 cup corn oil
1 tablespoon dry mustard
3/4 cup white vinegar
1 teaspoon salt
1 small onion, chopped
1/2 teaspoon celery seed

Put all in blender, blend well. Keeps well stored in refrigerator.

Sweet Sour Dressing

1 cup vinegar
1 cup sugar
1 cup water
1/3 cup oil
1/2 teaspoon garlic salt, optional

Shake in jar and pour over lettuce salad.

With two eyes and one tongue, you should see twice as much as you say.

Our Scandinavian
Heritage & More

Measurement And Conversion Chart

Metric To US
1 teaspoon in Sweden = 1/2 teaspoon in US

Liquid:
1 deciliter = 3.39 fl. ounces

Dry:
1 Hg. = 100 grams
1 gram = .035274 ounces
1 gram = .0022046 Pounds
Sugar: 190 grams = 1 cup
Pd. Sugar: 130 grams = 1 cup
Br. Sugar: 200 grams = 1 cup
Flour: 130 grams = 1 cup

US to Metric

Liquid:
1 cup = 2.37 deciliters
1 pint = 4.73 deciliters

Dry:
1 ounce = 30 grams
1 pound = 450 grams
To convert ounces to grams, multiply ounces x 28.35
To convert pounds to grams, multiply pounds x 453.59

Temperature conversions
Celsius to Fahrenheit

165 = 325
175 = 350
205 = 400

Grandma Hazel's Swedish Rye Bread

4 cups hot water (or part milk)
5 tablespoons shortening
2 tablespoons molasses (light)
1 tablespoon salt
1/2 - 3/4 cup sugar
2-1/2 teaspoons yeast or 2 packages
light rye flour
3 cups white flour
6 - 8 cups flour

Mix together the hot water, shortening, molasses, salt, sugar and yeast. Add enough light rye flour to give the batter a light beige color, I use a mixer for this part. Add the 3 cups white flour, it should be quite a heavy consistency. Pour batter into a trench (6 - 8 cups) of white flour. Knead in the flour until you can push your finger in and a hold stays. Let rise until it has doubled. Punch it down and knead for another 10 minutes. The more you knead the better the bread. Put into loaves, and let it rise again until doubled, about 2 hours. Bake at 350° for about 45 minutes. Makes about 3 loaves.

Lefse

5 cups potatoes, riced
1 teaspoon salt
2 tablespoons lard, melted
1 - 2 tablespoons milk
1 cup flour

Rice potatoes and mix in salt and melted lard. Add milk. Stir in flour. Knead together on a board. Roll into a 3 inch round roll, then slice about 1 inch thick. Chill. Remove only one slice at a time. Roll out on a floured surface until very thin. Put onto an electric griddle on high and bake until brown spots appear and steaming stops. Lift gently and turn to the other side and bake. Watch carefully.

Gunga's Raisin Bread

I watched Gunga make this, so a lot of this is in "abouts", but give it a try, it's well worth the effort. (My grandma Hansen was lovingly known as "Gunga".)

3 cups milk
1-3/4 - 2 sticks margarine
3/4 - 1 cup sugar
2 egg yolks, optional
4 - 5 cups flour
1 tablespoon salt
1 - 2 tablespoons cardamom
2 packages yeast
4 - 5 cups flour
1 cup raisins
1/2 cup citron

Warm together the milk, margarine, sugar and eggs. Mix the flour, salt, cardamom and yeast with the milk mixture. Make a trench on counter with the 4 - 5 cups of flour. Pour batter into trench carefully and knead gently. You may need a little more flour. Knead about 10 minutes. Put into a greased bowl and let rise in a warm place until doubled. Stir down in bowl and gently stir in raisins and citron. Shape into loaves, (you might want to braid some). Let rise in pans until doubled. About 1 hour. Bake at 350° for 30 to 45 minutes.

Gunga's Raisin Bread (Next Generation)

3 cups buttermilk
2 sticks butter
1 cup sugar
1-1/2 to 2 tablespoons fresh ground cardamom
2 egg yolks
2-1/4 teaspoons yeast
9 cups flour
raisins and citron, optional

Bring the buttermilk, butter, sugar, cardamom, egg yolks and yeast to just below boiling (120-130°). Mix into 4 cups flour for a soft sponge. Set this aside and let it rise for 30 to 45 minutes. Make a trench on the counter with at least 5 more cups of flour. Add soft sponge to the trench. Mix together and knead for about 10 minutes. Place in a large greased bowl. Cover, and let rise until doubled in a warm place. Punch down and gently add raisins and citron (if desired). Shape into loaves (I like to braid some). Let rise in pans until doubled. At least 1 hour. Bake at 350° for 30-45 minutes. We decided that 40 minutes was best and we used 3 x 7 inch pans.

Poteca

This variation came from Clara Bosanic. Very good.

> 1 loaf frozen bread dough, rolled out thin
>
> Filling:
> 1/4 cup soft butter
> 1/2 cup brown sugar
> 1/4 cup honey
> 1 egg
> 1/4 cup milk
> 1/2 teaspoon vanilla
> 2 cups walnut, finely ground

Mix filling and spread evenly over dough. Roll up, put in long bread pan. Bake at 325° for 45 to 50 minutes or until brown.

Poteca (Popetiza)

This is Molly's recipe that came from Frank's family.

> 1 stick margarine, melted
> 2 eggs
> 1/2 cup sugar (a healthy one)
> 1 tablespoon salt
> 1 package yeast dissolved in 2 cups warm water

Into these ingredients add 6 cups flour, 3 cups with a mixer and 3 cups by hand. Cover and refrigerate overnight. Flour counter well, let dough rest there until room temperature. Roll out approximately 24 x 30. Cover with this filling:

> 1 pound and 1 cup walnuts, finely chopped
> 1/2 cup sugar
> 1 stick margarine
> 4 eggs added last

Sprinkle with cinnamon and roll up. Put in pan in a horseshoe. Rise until not quite double. Bake at 350° for 30 minutes. Then turn down to 325° and bake for 15 minutes.

Limpa Bread

2 cups potato water
1 cup mashed potatoes
1-1/2 tablespoons each anise and caraway seeds
2 cups rye flour
1/4 cup molasses
2 cups water
5 tablespoons bacon grease
1 tablespoon salt
1 cup brown sugar
1 package yeast, dissolved in 1/2 glass warm water
2 cups sour milk or buttermilk
11 cups flour

Bring the potato water, potatoes, anise and caraway seeds to a boil and add the flour. Set aside, covered overnight. Mix in the molasses, water, bacon grease, salt, sugar, yeast, buttermilk and flour. Knead dough very well, 10-15 minutes at least. Let rise until doubled. Shape into loaves and poke holes in each loaf with a fork. Let rise again. Bake at 375° for 40 to 45 minutes. Hot from the oven, brush with the following mixture: (very important) extremely strong coffee made extremely sweet.

Krummel Torte

Sister Ludmilla Gramann shared this family recipe with me.

4 eggs, beaten
1 cup sugar
1 cup bread crumbs
1 teaspoon baking powder
1 cup dates, chopped
1 cup walnuts, chopped
canned fruit, drained
1 pint cream, whipped
bananas or strawberries, or both, sliced

Mix eggs and sugar. Add bread crumbs and baking powder. Fold in dates and nuts. Bake in a 9 x 9 inch pan for 40 minutes at 325°. Crumble the cake on a large torte plate. Cover with the canned fruit, any fruit you like, for example: peaches, pineapple or fruit cocktail. Top with cream. Top all with bananas, strawberries or both. The cake itself would make a very good bar.

Swedish Tea Log

1 package dry yeast, dissolved in 1/4 cup warm water. Set aside.
Sift together: 2-1/4 cups flour
2 tablespoons sugar
1 teaspoon salt
Cut into mixture: 1/2 cup margarine
Add: 1/4 cup evaporated milk
1 beaten egg

Add yeast to the above mixture and chill at least 2 hours or overnight. Divide dough into 3 rounds. Roll each out into a 12 x 6 rectangle and spread with 1/3 or the following mixture: 1/2 cup margarine and 1 cup brown sugar. Sprinkle with chopped walnuts. Roll up from long side and seal. Put on foil lined cookie sheet in a crescent shape. Make cuts along the edges. Let rise until light, an hour or so. Bake at 350° for 20-25 minutes. Frost while warm with the following glaze:

Melt 2 tablespoons butter and add 1 cup sifted powdered sugar and 1/2 teaspoon vanilla. Stir in milk to spreading constancy. Optional, decorate with red and green cherries.

Krumkage

This is a wonderful Norwegian cookie. It was a must at Christmas time. They're made on an iron, one at a time. They look like little lacy doilies all rolled up.

6 eggs, beaten until light
1 cup sugar
1/2 pound butter, melted
1 cup flour + 1 tablespoon
2 teaspoons ground cardamom

Mix well together. You may use vanilla, rum or brandy to flavor the batter. Heat iron to medium-hot and drop batter by tablespoon in center of iron. Close and wait about 30 seconds. Turn iron and check every few seconds for color. You don't want them too brown. Remove cookie from iron and immediately wrap around a dowel the size of a broomstick. Wait a few seconds and remove and cool. They're fragile.

Christmas Rice

This is a wonderful Norwegian tradition. My grandmother Kathinka Hansen brought it over from Norway with her and we have celebrated Christmas Eve this way since I was born. Since grandma's been gone, my mom has carried on the tradition. I hope it goes on forever.

```
3 cups rice
1 gallon milk, divided
a little salt shaken over the rice
1-1/2 tablespoons sugar
1 almond
```

Cover the rice well with milk. Add salt and sugar and cook very slowly (this scorches very easily.) As the mixture thickens, add a little more milk and stir. In all, you will use about 1 gallon of milk, and it will take about 2 hours to finish. When it's done and you're ready to serve it, drop a whole peeled almond into the rice and stir it in. Serve the rice in sauce dished with a dot of butter and cinnamon and sugar. This is always served as a first course, and the one who gets the almond gets a prize. In our house it's anything from $1.00 to a roll of toilet paper! GOD BLESS TRADITION!

Swedish Tea Log II

This comes from my Swedish friend Karin Sjogren.

```
1 cup flour
1/2 cup margarine
2 tablespoons water
1/2 cup butter
1 cup water
1 cup flour
3 eggs
1 teaspoon vanilla
```

Mix the flour, margarine and 2 tablespoons water like a pie crust, then divide in two. Press onto cookie sheet in long strips about 4 inches wide. Melt butter and 1 cup water. Simmer, then add flour and stir well. Add eggs, one at a time. Stirring well and quickly and add vanilla. Spread on top of crust and bake at 425° for 20 minutes. Shut off oven and leave for 10 more minutes. Top with the Butter Cream Frosting that follows.

Butter Cream Frosting

1-1/2 to 2 cups powdered sugar
1 stick margarine
1/2 cup shortening
1 teaspoon almond extract
1/4 cup cream (carnation or regular milk if you are in a pinch)

Beat well, full speed. Frost and sprinkle with almonds.

Gunnar's Cinnamon Rolls-Log-Braid

My cousin Gunnar from Sweden has wound his way around the hearts of even the smallest members of my family. We're all excited when we hear he's coming to visit. This is his recipe.

Filling:
3.5 ounces butter
1/2 cup sugar
4 tablespoons cinnamon
1 tablespoon vanilla

5.3 ounces butter
.13 gal. milk
1 package (cube) yeast 1.76 ounce
1/2 cup sugar
1/2 teaspoon salt
2 teaspoon cardamom
30 ounces flour

Mix filling ingredients together and set aside.

Melt butter in pan, add milk and heat to 98.6 on thermometer. In a large bowl break up yeast and add liquid gradually to dissolve yeast. Mix dry ingredients and slowly add to liquid. Keep out about 3/4 cup flour for rolling. Mix these ingredients for 5 minutes and let rise, covered for 40 minutes. Put 1/2 of the dough on a floured surface. Divide in half. Roll each half in a 14 x 16 rectangle. Divide filling into 4 even amounts and spread over rolled dough. Fold in half the long way and cut into 10 pieces. Twist the pieces to make a knot. Put on a greased cookie sheet, cover and let rise for 30 minutes.

Beat an egg and brush on knots, sprinkle with coarse sugar. Bake at 450° for 10 minutes. Cool on rack, covered until serving.

Morotskaka

This carrot cake is from my cousin Bjarne's wife Gunnel.

2 ägg
2 dl. socker
100 gr. smör
3 dl. Fint hackade morötter
2.5 dl. Vetemjöl
1.5 Tesked bakpulver
1 Tesked kanel
1 Tesked vaniljsocker

Blanda och gradda 40 minutes at 175° C.

English Translation - Carrot Cake

2 eggs
3/4 cup sugar
3-1/2 ounces butter
about 1-1/4 cup shredded carrots
1 cup flour
3/4 teaspoons baking powder
1/2 teaspoon cinnamon
1/2 teaspoon vanilla sugar

Mix together and bake at 350° for 40 minutes. I would use a 9 x 13 inch pan.

Children may tear up a house, but they can never break up a home.

Rabarber paj (crumbled pies)

4 stalk rabarber or also + 1 big fresh aple
2 cups vetemjöl
1 Tablespoon socker
3.5 ounces Margarin
1/2 C. sugar
1 tablespoon potato flour
Mix together and set aside.

Cut the rabarber and aple. Put in a paj form sprayed with grease. Mix 1/2 C. sugar with 1 tablespoon potato flour. Sprinkle over rabarber. Crumble flour mixture on top.

Bake 175 C. for 30-40 minutes. Our Cousin Inger served this when we were in Sweden. It was very good.

English Translation - Rhubarb Tart

This is a thin rhubarb dessert.

2 cups flour
1 tablespoon sugar
almost 1/2 stick margarine
4 stalks rhubarb, sliced
1 large apple, sliced, if desired
1/2 cup sugar
1 tablespoon potato flour, or another thick flour

Mix together the flour, sugar and margarine, until crumbly and set aside.

Place rhubarb and apple in greased pie tin. Mix sugar with flour and sprinkle over the fruit. Top with the crumble mixture. Bake at 350° for 30-40 minutes.

Kuklanekake

This is from cousin Jorunn in Norway.

6 egg og 7 dl. Farin piskes til eggdosis.
150 gr. Smør smeltes, avkjøles og tilsettes eggedosis dryppvis.
300 gr. Malte hasselnøtter, 275 gr. Hv. Mel og 2 ts. Bakepulver blandes i. Stekes in langpanne 200 I ca. 20-25 minutes.
På toppen
2 store pl. Helnott, 1 kopp fløte, 1 kopp meierismør smeltes I en kjele og helles på kaken mens den er litt lunken.

English Translation - Kuklanekake

Mix together: 6 eggs and 3 scant cups sugar
Then drizzle 10 tablespoons melted butter over egg mixture.
Add 1-1/3 cups ground hazelnuts, 1-1/4 cups flour and 2 teaspoons baking powder.
Pour into greased pan and bake at 375-400° for 20-25 minutes.

Topping:
Melt together: 1 cup cream, 1 cup butter and large chocolate bar with nuts. Pour over warm cake.

Classic Swedish Cake (Torte)

Blend together:
3 eggs
2-1/2 dl. sugar, (1-1/4 cups)
Add:
2-1/2 dl. flour, (1-1/4 cups)
1/2 dl. potato starch, (3-1/3 tbls.)
2 ts. baking powder
1 ts. vanilla and last, 3/4 dl. boiling water, (about 1/3 cup)

Mix well, pour into a 9 or 10 inch springform pan. Bake at 350° for 35 minutes. Cool cake completely. Cut across into 3 even layers. Put first layer on plate and cover with Custard (thicker version of vanilla sauce). Top with second cake layer. Top this with berries of your choice. Put on top layer and cover with whipped cream and decorate with more berries.

Chocolate Torte

Our cousins Egil and Lis sent this one. Lis makes wonderful desserts.

Mix 4 eggs with 150 gr. socker. (beat it for about 15 min.) Gently put in 150 gr. Vetemjöl. Put into a round form pan and bake at 200 for about 25 minutes.

Chocolate filling:
Boil up 1 dl. Water with 3/4 dl. Socker and put in 150gr. Plain chocolate. Cool and put in 1/4 liter whipped cream. For decorating, use kernel of nuts or whatever you like.

English Translation - Chocolate Torte

Mix 4 eggs with about 2/3 cup sugar. Beat for about 15 minutes. Slowly add about 2/3 cup flour. Pour into a springform pan and bake for about 25 minutes at 375°.

Chocolate filling:
Boil about 1/2 cup water and about 1/3 cup sugar. Add 5 ounces block chocolate (probably semi-sweet) and melt. Fold in 1 healthy cup whipped cream. Pour over cake layer. Refrigerate, remove from pan and decorate with nuts or whatever you like.

Chokladfudge

Cousin Gunnel from Sweden sent this. Chocolate, Mmmm.

Först skall detta blandes, smältas och rores på spisen:
1 dl. Grädde
2 dl. Socker
50 gr. Margarin
Blanda sedan i:
1 hg mörk blockchoklad
1 tsk snabbkaffe (pulverkaffe)
12 bitar marshmallows (vet ej stavning)
De skall vara sockerbitstora. En vanlig fyrkant klippes i 4 bitar.
Skall sjuda tills allt är smält. Ej kokas

Hälles I en liten form ca 18 x 12 cm, med smörpapper in botten. Skäres upp med
Kniv efter stelning ca 2 x 1 cm. skall bli 40 st. Om stelning uteblir- ät upp med sked.
Lika gott, men farligare för figuren.

English Translation - Chocolate Fudge

1/2 scant cup whipping cream
7-ounces (between 3/4 and 1 cup) sugar
3-1/2 tablespoons margarine

Stir together in pan until melted.

Then add:
About 3-1/2 ounces dark block chocolate
1/2 teaspoon Instant coffee
12 marshmallows, cut in quarters. About the size of a sugar cube. It's a
little larger than ours.

Cook together in a saucepan until melted. Don't boil. Put into a 5 x 7 inch pan lined
with parchment paper to set. Cut into small pieces. (About 40 pieces, 3/4 inch.) Sometimes it doesn't set so you have to eat it with a spoon. Good! But not good for the figure.

Saftiga Kokoskakor

My cousin, Gunnar loves these cookies, and his father, Frank made them too.

Blanda en pase kokosflingor (200 gr or 5 dl.) med l dl. Vaniljkräm, 1.5dl. socker och 1 ägg. Lägg klickar av smeten (ca 1 matsked) på plåt med bakplåtspapper och grädda in 200 I 12-15 minuter. Förvara kakorna in en bark tillsammans med en bit mjukt bröd så att de håller sig mjuka.

English Translation - Coconut Cookies

Mix 1 bag of coconut flakes with about 1/2 cup vanilla cream*, about 2/3 cup sugar and 1 egg. *(Vanilla cream is similar to our instant pudding mix. It can be purchased in markets that carry Scandinavian foods. If you use this product, mix 2-1/2 tablespoons vanilla powder with 1 dl. (1/2 scant cup milk). I'll follow this with a recipe for vanilla sauce to make from scratch. Drop this mixture on a greased cookie sheet by tablespoons and bake at 375° for 12-15 minutes. Store in a container with a slice of soft bread to insure the cookies will stay soft.

Vanilla Cream (Sauce)

To use this in the above recipe, you'll have to use less milk, maybe 1/2.

2 tablespoons sugar
1-1/2 teaspoons cornstarch
2 cups milk
3 egg yolks
1 teaspoon vanilla

Mix together sugar and cornstarch. Stir in milk and cook, stirring constantly until sauce thickens. Reduce heat to very low and cook for 8 minutes, letting the sauce bubble now and then. Add some of the hot sauce to the egg yolks and mix well. Add rest of the hot sauce and combine. Cook 2 minutes more. Remove from the heat and add the vanilla.

Mazarinbitar

This is a very good bar from Inger (Arvid) Flygh

1 ägg
1.5 dl. Socker
1.5 dl. Mjölk
150 gr. Melted smör
1.5 ts. bakpulver
2-1/4 dl. vetemjöl
1 Tbls. Vanilla socker
25 (0.5 dl.) hackad mandlar.
bittermandel

Mix ägg, socker, mjölk och smör. Add dry ingredients. Put into square cake pan. Bake at 175 for 30 minutes.

Glaze with:
2 dl. flor socker
2 Tbls. vatten
1 - 2 drops grön mat färg

English Translation - Green Frosted Cake Bars

Mix together:
1 egg
about 2/3 cup sugar
about 2/3 cup milk
10 tablespoons margarine, melted

Add:
3/4 teaspoons baking powder
1 healthy cup flour
1 tablespoon vanilla sugar
4 tablespoons ground almonds

Bitter almond cannot be purchased in the US. I just add more almond. Bake at 350° for about 35-30 minutes. Glaze with: about 3/4 cup powdered sugar, 2 tablespoons water and 1 - 2 drops of green food coloring.

Finska pinnar

Arvid's wife Inger made these cookies when we were there. I make them every Christmas.

> 200 gr. Smör
> 50 gr socker
> 3 - 6 rivna bittermandlar
> 225 gr vetemjöl
>
> Until penslig 1 äggvita
> Pärlsocker
> 10 hackade sotmandler

Rör smör och socker. Rör in riven bittermandel. Blanda i vetemjöl och rulla ut i stänger. Skär stängerna i 5 - 6 cm. Långa bitar och pensla med äggvita. Doppas i pärlsocker och hackad sötmandel. Sätts in i 225-250 C tills de får rätt färg.

English Translation - Almond Cookies

> 14 tablespoons butter
> 3-1/2 tablespoons sugar
> 3 - 6 grated bitter almonds (This product is not sold in the US,
> so you may substitute 1 - 2 teaspoons almond extract.)
> 1-1/2 cups + 3/4 tablespoon flour

Mix together and roll into a rope about the size of your little finger. Cut into 2 - 3 inch lengths. Brush with egg whites and dip into finely chopped almonds and pearl sugar. Bake at 350° for 12-15 minutes.

Uppsala Cake

This lovely cake also came from cousin Inger in Sweden.

> 4 eggs
> 1 cup sugar (white)
> 2 cups nuts (hazel)
> 1-1/2 cups almonds (ground)

Beat the eggs and sugar. Add the ground hazelnut and almonds. Put into a round cake pan and bake for 20-25 minutes at 325°. Frost with créme fraiche and a mixture of berries.

Double Good Pastries
This is another of Inger's good ones.

Dough:
200 gr. almonds, (3/4 cup)
5 dl. powdered sugar, (2 healthy cups)
4 egg whites

Filling Cream:
1 dl. strong cold coffee, (1 scant cup)
1 tablespoon flour
1 egg yolk
125 gr. butter, (4 ounces)
3/4 dl. powdered sugar, (1/3 cup)
1/2 teaspoon vanilla sugar

Grind almonds and blend with the sugar. Whisk egg whites until stiff and fold gently into sugar-almond mixture. Spoon by teaspoon onto a parchment paper covered cookie sheet. Bake at 350° for 8-10 minutes.

Mix the coffee and the flour in a saucepan. Let it simmer to a cream. Stir the egg yolk into it and let it cool just a little. Then blend the butter, sugar and vanilla in a cup and then mix it into the coffee cream. Put together the small cakes with a big portion of cream between them. To serve them cold is the most superb cakes. They can be frozen for quite a long time.

Potato Sausage
This wonderful recipe came from Amanda Carlstrom years ago and I make it every year on Christmas Eve.

1/2 pound pork casings
2 pounds ground beef
2 pounds ground pork, I have the meat ground together in the meat department.
12 cups ground raw potatoes
4 medium onions, ground
12 teaspoons salt
3 teaspoons white pepper

Mix all ingredients together well, then fill casings, loosely. To cook, prick all over with a needle, then simmer (do not boil) for 45 minutes. If you boil it hard it will break.

Ginger Loaf

My cousin Nancy in Norway gave me this. She's British you know, and I think this is too.

10 ounces flour
1/2 teaspoon baking soda
1/2 teaspoon salt
2 tablespoons cinnamon
2 tablespoons ground ginger
6 ounces brown sugar
2 ounces black treacle (dark molasses)
2 ounces golden syrup
6 ounces butter
2 eggs
Warm milk for mixing

Sift flour, soda, salt, cinnamon and ginger together. Stir in brown sugar. Cream molasses, syrup and butter until light and fluffy. Add eggs, one at a time, beating well after each addition. Fold flour mixture in folding to a stiff consistency alternately with the warm milk. Spoon into a 2 pound bread tin lined with paper and bake in a 350° oven for about 2 hours. After 20 minutes, put on wire rack to cool. Decorate with preserved ginger. Store in airtight container. This cake should be kept for at least a week before eating.

Rulapulsa

This is a pressed Christmas meat that has come down through the generations on the Norwegian side of my family. It's typed exactly as my father has passed it on.

2 beef flanks with a little meat on for the jacket. Sew 2 together with crochet cotton if need be. Spread saltpeter on with fingers. (This reddens the meat). Then salt and pepper, LOTS OF IT. Next comes strips of pork placed on flank. Then strips of beef. Put chopped onions on the beef, then strips of veal. Put more beef on top and then more pork. More salt and pepper and onions. Keep on filling until the jacket or flank will be tight. When it's all together, sew her up! Rub saltpeter on the outside. Put into a crock, with lots of salt, top and bottom. Leave it for 9 days. Keep turning over in the crock so it sets in its brine. After 9 days roll in a cheesecloth bag and boil gently for 4 hours. Put under a press until cool. Slice very thin to serve.

Liver Pate

Åsa, Gunnar's sister shared this recipe of their mom's.

200 gr. margarine, (14 tablespoons)
500 gr. beef liver, (1 pound, 2-ounces)
5 filets of anchovies
1 yellow onion
3 tablespoons flour
2-1/2 dl. milk, (1 healthy cup)
3 eggs
1 teaspoon salt
1/4 teaspoon white pepper
1/4 teaspoon allspice
1/8 teaspoon cloves

Melt margarine, cool. Rinse liver in cold water. Grind or process liver, anchovies, and onion. Add flour to 1/2 the milk and whisk until smooth. Add eggs, and then add the rest of the milk. Mix spices, margarine and egg mixture into liver. Put about 4.5 dl. (or 2-1/4 cups) of the mixture into foil pans about 2 inch high. Bake at 350 for 1 hour. Can freeze in pans and bake later.

Summer Salmon Dish

My cousin Jorunn Vestlie in Norway made this and it is beautiful as well as delicious.

Salt 5 salmon steaks. Refrigerate for an hour or so. Poach the steaks in a large pan on stove top. When they begin to flake, remove and cool. Break into pieces and spread on platter. Top with 1 large can drained pineapple tidbits and 1 jar of white asparagus, cut up.

Mix together equal amounts of mayonnaise and whipped cream, about 2 cups each. Add the juice of 1/2 lemon, salt and pepper to taste, chives and dill if desired. Jorunn said dill doesn't go with salmon, but I like it. Frost salmon with this mixture and garnish with hard boiled egg and tomato wedges and parsley. This was served with crusty bread and it was great.

Rømmegrøt

This dish is truly a heart attack in a bowl, but well loved by Norwegians. Cousin Vestla gave me the recipe.

Ingredienser:
6 dl. Seterrømme
ca 2 dl. Hvetemel
ca 5 dl. Melk
1/2 ts. Salt

Kok rommen under lokk I ca 2 min.

Varm opp melken

Rør halvparten av hvetemelet inn I rommen.

Rør krafig until smøret pipler frem.

Skum av smøret.

Rør inn resten av melen og spe med melken. La koke under jevn omrøring ca 5 min.

Smak until med salt.

Server med smøret, sucker og kanel.

English Translation - Rømmegrøt

2-1/2 cups sour cream
about 3/4 cup flour
about 2 cups milk
1/2 teaspoon salt

Boil the sour cream under a lid for about 2 minutes. Warm the milk. Stir 1/2 the flour into the sour cream. Stir well until the butter comes to the top. Skim the butter and put to one side. Stir the remainder of the flour into the sour cream and add the milk a little at a time. Simmer while stirring for about 5 minutes. Add salt and stir. To serve top with some of the butter and sprinkle with sugar and cinnamon.

Au Gratin Potatoes From Jorunn

Butter a Casserole or a 9 x 13 inch pan. Layer sliced potatoes and sliced onions alternately. Sprinkle a little fresh minced or grated garlic in each layer along with salt and pepper. Top with heavy cream (about 2 cups) and shredder Jarlsberg cheese. Bake at 325° for about 45 minutes.

Resisting temptation is usually just a matter of putting it off until nobody's looking.

Good Luncheon Quiche

Inger (Arvid) Flygh made this for us and we couldn't get enough.

Pre-bake a pie crust (deep dish) according to directions.
1/4 cup chopped green onions
1 shallot, thinly sliced
1 leek, thinly sliced
3/4 cup crisp bacon or ham
1 cup good Swiss cheese (I prefer Gruyere or Jarlsberg)
3 eggs
1 cup cream or créme fraiche
salt and pepper to taste

Sauté all the onion. Layer onion mixture and bacon or ham in the baked pie shell. Cover with the cheese. Mix the eggs, cream, salt, pepper and pour over other ingredients. Bake at 325° for 45 to 60 minutes. Watch carefully and make sure it's completely set. Top with more cheese if you desire. Let set for about 20 minutes in a warm place before serving. (I sometimes layer strips of roasted red pepper on top of the onion layer for added flavor.)

Pierogi

This wonderful Polish dish was taught to me by a friend, Connie Nault from Lower Michigan. This is a recipe that was handed down, so there are a lot of "abouts".

Put about 5 pounds of flour in a very large bowl and make a hole in the center. Break 5 eggs (jumbo) into the hole and sprinkle with salt. Put 2 - 3 heaping tablespoons sour cream in as well. Start adding water gradually, and mix with hands from the center of the ingredients. Continue to add water until all the flour is incorporated and you have a soft dough. Let dough set for a few minutes.

Filling #1
   Open 6 regular size cans of Franks Bavarian style sauerkraut. Sauté in a large pan with 3 sticks butter. Add 6 small cans of sliced mushrooms and 1 sweet onion, diced. Season with salt and pepper.

Filling #2
   Boil potatoes in salted water. Mash with diced onions that have been sautéed in butter. Add cheese, lots of it and salt and pepper. If desired, you can add some sour cream.

Flour a large surface, break off a piece of the dough. Roll out very thin. Cut circles about 4 inches across. Fill each circle with about 2 tablespoons filling. Fold in half and pinch and turn edges all around. Put in boiling water until they rise to the top. Stir gently and let cook 3-4 minutes more. Remove to a sheet pan and brush liberally with butter to prevent sticking. These freeze very well. Before serving, sauté them in butter till golden. I put some shredded pork in the sauerkraut filling. It was awesome.

Soups & Sandwiches

Potato Soup

Jumbo Hoholik brought this recipe to work. Several of us tried it. It's very rich and very good.

1 large can chicken broth
1 onion, chopped
8 cups raw potatoes, diced
1-1/2 pounds bacon, cooked crispy and diced
1-1/2 8-ounce packages cream cheese
1 large can of cream of chicken soup
8 ounces sour cream
salt to taste
few dashes of pepper

Combine broth, onion and potatoes. Bring to a boil, reduce heat and simmer 10 minutes or until potatoes are tender. Place half of this mixture in blender and process 30 seconds, then put all the mixture together again. Add crisp bacon and remaining ingredients. Stir and simmer until everything is well blended.

Cheesy Chowder

1 cup raw potatoes, chopped
1 cup raw carrots, chopped
1/4 cup onion, diced
1 tablespoon butter
3 cups chicken broth
dash of pepper
4 tablespoons margarine
1/2 cup flour
2 cups milk
1-1/4 cups Velveeta® cheese, cubed
2 tablespoons parsley

In large pot cook potatoes, carrots and onions in butter until done, not brown. Add broth and pepper. Cover and simmer for about 30 minutes. Make a basic white sauce with margarine, flour and milk. Stir until thick and add to chowder with the cheese and parsley. Stir until cheese melts. You can make this a great broccoli soup by adding a package of frozen broccoli cuts. And maybe a little ham.

Vegetable Beef Soup

a good size package boneless beef short ribs
8 cups beef broth
potatoes
carrots
onion
celery
cabbage
rutabaga
1 small can diced tomatoes
1 - 1-1/2 cups cooked barley
salt and pepper
1 bay leaf

In a large pot, simmer short ribs in the beef broth. While that cooks, using a coarse grind, chop potatoes, carrots, onions, celery, a little cabbage and a little rutabaga. Add to the pot and continue cooking. Add tomatoes and cooked barley. Then just salt, pepper and bay leaf. When the meat is tender, remove from the pot, cool and cut in small pieces. Put back in the pot and enjoy. It's great. My grandma didn't like her veggies ground, so she chopped them by hand.

Pea Soup

ham bone
water
onion, chopped
1 small bag yellow or green split peas
potatoes, chopped
carrots, chopped
celery, chopped
salt and pepper

Cover the ham bone with water in a large pot with onion and simmer for at least 30 minutes. Add split peas and continue cooking. Stir once in a while so the peas don't stick on the bottom. Add the potatoes, carrots and celery to the soup. When the ham is tender, take the bone out and cool it. Take the ham off the bone and return to the pot. Cook until the peas are all cooked and have dissolved. I just use salt and pepper, but some people like thyme. This soup will be richer if you use chicken stock instead of water.

Pumpkin Soup

Sister Ludmilla served this soup at a retirement party and it was the hit of the night.

> 1 large onion, diced
> 2 - 3 teaspoons fresh garlic, minced
> 4 tablespoons butter
> 1/8 teaspoon cayenne pepper
> 1/8 teaspoon coriander
> 1/8 teaspoon curry powder
> 1 large can solid pack pumpkin
> 2-1/2 cups chicken broth
> 1/2 cup brown sugar
> 1 cup heavy cream

Sauté onion and garlic in butter. Add spices and stir well. Add pumpkin and broth. Heat and blend until smooth (in blender). Put back in soup pot and add brown sugar. Heat on low and add the cream just before serving. This soup is presented in… you guessed it… a pumpkin.

Level the bottom of the pumpkin. Remove the top and clean out insides. Spray the inside and the outside with a pan spray, turn the top upside down on the pumpkin and turn the entire pumpkin upside down on a cookie sheet that has been sprayed. Bake in a 350° oven for 45 minutes. Remove from oven, cool, turn upright and fill with hot soup. Serve each bowl with a little dollop of sour cream and a spoonful of crisp bacon bits. It's soooo good.

Stuffed Green Pepper Soup

> 1 to 1-1/2 pounds lean ground beef
> 1 medium onion, diced
> 1 cup green pepper, diced
> 2 cups beef stock
> 1 can diced tomatoes with basil and garlic
> 1 jar of chunky spaghetti sauce
> 3/4 - 1 package long grain and wild rice

Brown ground beef with onion and green pepper. To this add beef stock, tomatoes and spaghetti sauce. Simmer and add rice. If it gets too thick, add a little tomato juice. This is a very hearty soup.

Chili

> 2 pounds ground beef
> 1 medium onion, chopped
> 1 large can chopped tomatoes
> 1 large can tomato sauce
> 1 small can tomato paste
> 1 tomato paste can of water
> 1 can chili beans
> 1 can dark red kidney beans
> chili powder to taste

Brown ground beef with onion in a large pot. When browned, add chopped tomatoes, tomato sauce and tomato paste. Add water, simmer till tomato mixture is well blended. Then add chili beans and kidney beans, drain the beans just a little. (I like beans.) Then add the chili powder, get out the crackers and just graze. By the way, I have to have a glass of milk with my chili.

Borscht (Russian Beet Soup)

This is Gug's dear friend, Mary Moffat's recipe. She made it for us one summer and it was wonderful. Don't let the beet scare you.

> about 24 ounces tomato juice or V-8®
> 3 cans beets, drained and pureed
> 1 can chicken broth
> 1 dash lemon juice
> grated onion to taste
> allspice, grated, start with 1 tablespoon

Put all together, bring to a boil and simmer for about 10 minutes. Serve hot or cold. Garnish with sour cream and/or a slice of lemon.

*The Polish version of this soup has chopped cabbage and maybe some chopped potatoes.

Chicken Noodle Soup

This is a good, hearty soup, especially on a cold day.

1 cut up chicken
water or chicken stock
carrots
celery
onions
diced tomatoes
parsley
noodles

Cook chicken in water or chicken stock in a large pot until the meat is very tender. Remove and cool. Cut up carrots, celery and onions to desired size and put into the broth. I put some diced tomatoes and parsley in for flavor. You might find that you need a little chicken bouillon or soup base to enhance the flavor if you start with water. Take the chicken off the bones and put back into the pot and continue to simmer the soup. About 30 minutes before you serve, make noodles. You will find the recipe in the bread section. (Or use packaged pasta of your choice.) Add to the soup and serve.

Italian Soup

This is good and very healthy.

2 large onions, diced
2 tablespoons olive oil
4 cloves garlic, minced
6 cups chicken stock
1 28-ounce can petite diced tomatoes
1/4 - 1/3 cup fresh parmesan cheese, grated
1 cup cooked rice, can use more
2 chicken breast, cooked and diced
fresh basil

Gently sauté onions in olive oil. Stir occasionally for about 25 minutes. Add garlic, be careful not to burn. Add stock, tomatoes and parmesan cheese. When this is all blended together, add rice and chicken. Garnish with torn, fresh basil.

Grilled Corned Beef Sandwiches

1 can corned beef
onion, chopped, to taste
Swiss cheese, shredded (if you like lots, use lots. It's melty and great)
enough mayonnaise to hold together
sliced bread
egg
milk

Combine the first four ingredients and mix well. Spread some of the mixture between two slices of bread, dip the sandwich into a mixture of egg with a little milk and fry on both sides until golden and the cheese is melted. *This mixture heaped on a small crisped bread round and put under the broiler for a minute or so makes a great appetizer.

Baked Chicken Sandwiches

16 slices of bread with the crusts cut off
1-1/2 cups cooked chicken, cubed
1 can sliced water chestnuts
2 tablespoons onion, minced
2 tablespoons pimento
2 cans cream of celery soup
3 egg whites
2 tablespoons milk
crushed potato chips

Line a cookie sheet with 8 slices of the bread. Mix the chicken, water chestnuts, onion, pimento and soup together well and spread thickly on bread. Cover with remaining 8 slices of bread to make sandwiches. Cover and refrigerate overnight. To serve: beat egg whites with the milk and brush over the tops of sandwiches. Top with crushed potato chips. Bake 1 hour at 300°. Serve with fresh veggies, spiced apples, Jello® salad etc.

Bunsteads

My Grandma Hazel used to make these, and they've carried on for a couple of generations.

Make a tuna salad for sandwiches. Use only enough mayonnaise to hold the mixture together. Sometimes I add a hard boiled egg, chopped. Add some diced American cheese. Slightly hollow out a hamburger or hot dog bun. Heap some of the tuna mixture into the bun. Wrap with tin foil and put the bunsteads in the oven at about 400° for 15 to 20 minutes. They make a great lunch on a cold day.

Hot Beef Sandwiches

Either roast a pot roast and a chopped onion covered in the oven at about 325° until the meat falls apart (a couple of hours). Or cook the roast in a crock pot till the meat shreds. I think the oven method gives more flavor. Add a little water. I put an envelope of Au Jus mix in the water and let it cook a while longer. If you like it thickened a little more add a little flour and water mixture as you would for gravy. Season with salt and pepper. Serve on rolls. This is great for a crowd of people.

Sloppy Joes

This is a quick and very good recipe that came from the St. Patrick Circle at St. Francis.

2 pounds ground beef, browned
1 small onion, chopped
1/4 of a green pepper, chopped
1 can tomato soup
1 jar chili sauce

Mix well and cook till vegetables are done.

Creamed Tuna On Toast

1/2 cup butter
1/2 cup flour
2 cups milk
a dash of each: lemon juice, garlic powder, salt,
  pepper, paprika and Worcestershire sauce
2 cans tuna

To make the cream sauce, stir together the butter and flour in a pan over medium heat. Add milk slowly, stirring until thick. Add lemon juice, garlic powder, salt, pepper, paprika and Worcestershire sauce. Add tuna and heat together. I like to add peas. Spoon over toast and enjoy. No one can eat just one!! *Note: Use good tuna so it doesn't dissolve in the sauce.

Main Dishes

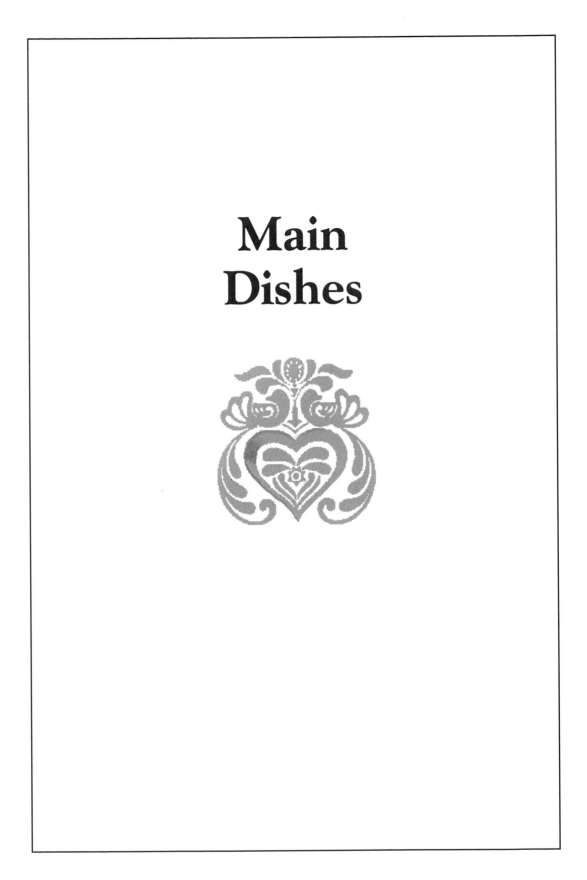

Center City Stew

Grandpa and Grandma Hansen wintered in Texas. On one trip there was a bad storm and they had to stop in a little Texas town called Center City. The only restaurant was only open for coffee. The owners offered them a bowl of stew they'd made for themselves. Thus-Center City Stew. This is made as well as we can remember and the amounts are negotiable.

1-1/2 to 2 onions, diced
3 cloves garlic, minced
1/2 pound salt pork, diced small
about 4 pounds beef (a chuck roast is good), cubed small and trimmed well
4 cups beef stock
about 2 cups water
lots of cracked pepper
potatoes, diced, as much as you like

Saute onions, garlic and salt pork until lightly brown. Cook beef in stock and water until it is tender, add onion mixture and pepper, add the potatoes last. Simmer until the potatoes are done. This is a hardy soup and is wonderful with crusty bread.

Stuffed Peppers

4 - 6 pepper halves
1-1/2 to 2 pounds ground beef
1 small onion, chopped
about 1-1/2 cups cooked rice
about 1/4 cup peppers, chopped
1 large can tomatoes, chopped
If it's too dry, add 1 small can tomato sauce or some tomato juice

Blanche peppers for 2-3 minutes. Brown ground beef, add onion, rice, peppers and tomatoes. Fill peppers and top with buttered bread crumbs or crushed potato chips. Bake at 350° for about 30 minutes.

Chop Suey

This is Gug's way of doing it and she made great chop suey.

1 - 1-1/2 pounds chop suey meat
onion, chopped
celery, chopped
butter
salt and pepper
soy sauce
brown gravy sauce or Kitchen Bouquet®
1 can bean sprouts, drained
1 can water chestnuts, drained
1 can bamboo shoots, drained
1 can mushrooms, drained

Brown chop suey meat, just cover with water and simmer. Sauté onion and celery in butter just until tender, add to the meat and continue simmering. Season with salt, pepper, soy sauce and brown gravy sauce or Kitchen Bouquet® for a rich brown color. When meat and vegetables are tender, add the bean sprouts, water chestnuts, bamboo shoots and mushrooms. Thicken with a little cornstarch and water. Serve with rice and some nice warm dinner rolls.

Mock Lasagna

2 pounds hamburger
1 medium onion, chopped
salt and pepper
spaghetti sauce (either homemade or readymade)
2 cups mozzarella cheese, shredded
2 cups cheddar cheese, shredded
1 package crescent rolls
8 ounces sour cream

Brown hamburger and chopped onion. Season with salt and pepper. Put into casserole dish, top with a favorite spaghetti sauce. Sprinkle with mozzarella and cheddar cheeses. Open crescent rolls and spread them with sour cream. Roll them back up into crescents and place them on top of cheese. Bake casserole at 350-375° for 45 minutes, or until rolls are golden brown.

Reuben Loaf

This lovely recipe from my friend Marta is a wonderful lunch or dinner loaf served with a salad. Also, the bread by itself is just great.

> 3 - 3-1/2 cups flour
> 1 package quick rise yeast
> 1 tablespoon sugar
> 1 tablespoon butter, softened
> 1 teaspoon salt
> 1 cup warm water
> 1/4 cup Thousand Island dressing
> 6 ounces shaved deli style corn beef
> 4 ounces Swiss cheese, shredded
> 1 8-ounce can sauerkraut, drained
> 1 egg white, beaten

Mix about 2-1/2 cups flour, yeast, sugar, butter and salt. Add water and mix to a soft dough. Flour a board with the rest of the flour and knead for about 4 minutes. Roll to a 14 x 10 inch rectangle and place on a sheet pan. Spread the center 1/3 of the dough with the Thousand Island dressing. Top with corned beef, Swiss cheese and sauerkraut. Make diagonal cuts, 1 inch apart down the sides of the dough and fold alternately over the filling to make a braided effect. Cover and let rest/rise for about 20 minutes in a warm place. Brush with the egg white and bake at 400° for 25 minutes or until golden brown. Serve warm and refrigerate leftovers.

Chinese Fried Rice

> 1/2 cup ham, cooked chicken or pork, diced
> 2 tablespoons oil
> 1 3-ounce can broiled mushrooms in steak sauce
> 1-1/2 tablespoons green onion, chopped
> 1 quart rice, cooked and cold
> 2 or 3 tablespoons soy sauce
> 1 egg, well beaten

Fry meat lightly; add mushrooms, green onion, rice and soy sauce. Continue to cook over low heat 10 minutes. Add egg, cook 5 minutes, stirring frequently. If darker color is desired, add more soy sauce.

Broccoli-Ham Ring

4 ounces (1/2 cup) deli ham, chopped
1 cup fresh broccoli, chopped (I blanche this for about 5 minutes)
1/4 cup onion, chopped
1/4 cup fresh parsley, chopped
1-1/2 cups Swiss or cheddar cheese, shredded
2 tablespoons dijon mustard
1 teaspoon lemon juice
2 8-ounce packages of crescent rolls

Mix all ingredients except crescent rolls and set aside. Arrange crescent triangles in a circle on a 13 inch baking stone or pizza pan, with bases overlapping in center, and points to the outside. There should be about a 3 inch diameter circle in center. Evenly spoon filling over the base. Fold points of triangles over filling and tuck under base at center. Filling will not be completely covered. Bake at 350° for 20-25 minutes or until golden brown. Makes 8 servings.

Pizza Bread
This came from Clara Bosanic. Very good!

1 loaf frozen bread dough, thawed
1 egg, beaten
1/4 pound ham, sliced thin
1/4 pound mozzarella cheese, sliced
1/4 pound salami, sliced
1/4 pound provolone cheese, sliced
1/4 pound pepperoni, sliced
Italian seasoning
parmesan cheese

Roll out bread dough thin and brush with egg. Layer on the bread the ham, mozzarella cheese, salami, provolone cheese and pepperoni. Sprinkle with seasoning and parmesan cheese. Roll up from the long side and pinch the seam. Put seam side down and brush with remaining egg. Bake at 350° for 35 minutes.

Tuna Ring

This is a wonderful family meal and it's pretty too.

> 1 egg
> 2 cans tuna, drained well (use the good stuff)
> 1/2 cup onion, chopped
> 1/2 cup cheddar cheese, shredded
> 1/2 cup fresh parsley, chopped, or 2 teaspoons parsley flakes
> 1 teaspoon celery salt
> 1/4 teaspoon pepper
> 2 cups Bisquick®
> 1/2 cup cold water

Beat egg slightly, take out 1 - 2 tablespoons for later. Stir tuna, onion, cheese, parsley, celery salt and pepper into remaining egg.

To prepare dough mix the Bisquick® and water together. Turn out onto a lightly floured surface and knead 5 times. Roll out to a 15 x 10 rectangle. Spread with tuna mixture. Roll up from the long side. With seam side down, shape into a ring and fasten the ends together. Make slashes in the top of ring at about 1 inch intervals about 2/3 of the way through the ring. Brush with remaining egg. Bake on a greased cookie sheet at 350° for 25 to 30 minutes. Serve with either a cream sauce with peas or a cheese sauce.

Basic Cream Sauce

> 1/4 cup margarine
> 1/4 cup flour
> 2 cups milk
> salt and pepper
> a dash of each: lemon juice, garlic powder, paprika and Worcestershire sauce

Melt margarine in saucepan. Add flour and stir well. Add milk slowly stirring constantly. Season with salt, pepper, lemon juice, garlic powder, paprika, and Worcestershire sauce.

To make a cheese sauce, just add about 1 to 1-1/2 cups shredded cheese.

Lasagna Bread

A nice main dish from Linda Parker.

1 pound ground beef
1/2 clove garlic, minced
1/2 teaspoon sweet basil
1/2 teaspoon salt
dash pepper
1 tablespoon parsley flakes
1/2 teaspoon oregano
3/4 cup onion, chopped
1 small can tomato paste
1 cup creamed cottage cheese
1/4 cup parmesan cheese
1 egg
2 cans crescent rolls
mozzarella cheese, sliced
1 tablespoon milk
sesame seeds, optional

Brown ground beef, add seasonings, onion and tomato paste. Mix well. Mix together cottage cheese, parmesan cheese and egg. On large sheet pan, press crescent rolls into a 15 x 13 rectangle. Put 1/2 meat mixture down center of rectangle. Cover with cottage cheese mixture, then the rest of the meat mixture, and top with mozzarella cheese. Fold the dough over the filling like an envelope. Brush with milk and sprinkle with sesame seeds. Bake at 375° for 25 minutes. Slice to serve.

Salmon Loaf Or Patties

1 can salmon, cleaned and broken
2 eggs, beaten
onion to taste
1/2 cup bread or cracker crumbs
1 teaspoon parsley
Salt and pepper to taste

Mix together and put into a greased bread pan. Bake at 350° for 1 hour. For patties, shape salmon mixture into patties and fry in butter until golden brown and crisp on both sides. The cream sauce recipe on page 85 with peas added, is great with this.

Salmon Or Fish Patties

canned fish (any kind you prefer)
potatoes, shredded
onion, grated
1 - 2 eggs
salt and pepper, to taste

The ingredient amounts are all up to your own taste. 1/2 to 1 cup potato is probably enough for a can of fish. Mix all together and shape into patties. Roll in flour and fry in butter or oil. I like a cream sauce with these.

Meatloaf Or Meatballs

2 pounds ground beef
2 eggs
2 slices bread soaked in milk or water, then broken into the meat
1 small onion, grated
salt and pepper
a dash each: garlic powder, paprika, dry mustard, oregano or sweet basil, parsley flakes
a dash allspice, optional

Mix together well with hand until it has a nice soft texture. Form into meatloaf and bake in a loaf pan or shape into meatballs and bake in a casserole. If you do meatballs, bake them in enough water to not quite cover the meat. Bake at 350° for about an hour. If you want a thicker gravy, mix a little flour in the water and add a little Kitchen Bouquet®. Mix with the meatballs and it will have a rich brown gravy.

Prime Rib (How to bake it, closed oven method.)

Place meat, (any size) uncovered, no water in a preheated 375° oven for 1 hour. Turn off oven. Do Not Open Oven!! About 1 hour before serving, turn the oven back on to 375° for 30-45 minutes. 30 minutes for rare, 45 minutes for medium rare.

Side Dishes & Sauces

Calico Beans

This is a very hardy dish. Great for picnics, camp, etc., but – watch for gas, it could carry you away.

> 1 16-ounce can pork and beans, undrained
> 1 16-ounce can butter beans, undrained
> 1 16-ounce can kidney beans, undrained
> 1 16-ounce can great northern beans, undrained
> 1/2 cup sugar
> 1/2 cup brown sugar
> 1/2 cup ketchup
> 1/2 pound bacon, browned, drained and diced
> 1/2 pound ground beef, browned and drained

Mix beans together and add the sugars, ketchup, bacon and ground beef. Mix together and bake uncovered for 1-1/2 hours at 325°.

In labors of love, every day is payday.

My Favorite Mac And Cheese

> 2-1/4 cup cheddar cheese, shredded
> 4 cups pasta, cooked and drained
> 3 eggs
> 3/4 cup light sour cream or créme fraiche
> 1/4 cup butter, cut in pieces
> dash of salt
> 1 hefty cup 2% milk

Mix cheese and hot pasta. Add remaining ingredients and put into a greased casserole dish. Bake at 350° for 30-45 minutes. Sprinkle top with a little more cheese and serve.

Sweet Potato Soufflé

I had this at a dinner theater and the chef was good enough to give me his recipe. I've tweaked it a little.

3 cups sweet potatoes, baked and mashed
1/2 cup butter, melted
1 scant cup sugar
2 beaten eggs
1/2 cup milk or cream
1/4 cup orange juice
1/2 - 1 teaspoon almond flavoring

Mix together and pour into greased casserole dish.

Top with:
1 cup brown sugar
1/2 cup flour
1/2 cup butter
1 cup pecans, chopped

Mix together in food processor until crumbly, add pecans. Sprinkle over casserole and bake at 350° for 45-50 minutes.

Twice Baked Potatoes

potatoes
1 egg
sour cream
bacon, crumbled
cheese
onions
paprika
parsley flakes
chives

Bake 1 more potato than you need, cut off tops and scoop out potatoes. Mash as you would ordinarily do, but add the egg. Add sour cream, bacon crumbles, cheese, onions or anything else you like. Fill the potato shells (heaping). Sprinkle with paprika, parsley flakes, chives etc. Bake at 375° for about 30 minutes.

Potato Puffs

cold mashed potatoes, they should be quite stiff
1 egg
onion, minced, to taste
green pepper, minced, to taste
salt and pepper, to taste
cheese, shredded
flour
1 egg, beaten
bread or cracker crumbs

Combine the first six ingredients and form into small balls (golf ball size). Roll in flour, then in the beaten egg and in bread or cracker crumbs. At this point, you can refrigerate them for a day if you need to, or they can be fried or deep fried at once. This is really a good change of pace potato dish.

Bread Stuffing

1-1/2 cups onion, chopped
1-1/2 cups celery, chopped
about 1/2 apple, chopped
2 sticks margarine
giblets, diced
Salt and pepper, to taste
1/2 teaspoon poultry seasoning
1/2 teaspoon sage
8 - 12 cups bread, broken in small pieces or dry bread cubes
chicken broth (if needed)

Sauté onions, celery and apple in margarine until tender. Add giblets (cooked). Season bread and pour onion mixture over it. This is when you would use the broth if you needed to. Combine and stuff turkey or put into a casserole.

Clam Stuffing

Judy McDonough gave me this too. Many times we hurried to get the crunchy edges.

3 pounds butter
4 - 6 onions, diced
1/4 cup parsley flakes
1 tablespoon seafood seasoning
2-1/2 large loaves bread, cubed
4 cans minced clams
4 eggs

Simmer, butter, onions, parsley and seasonings 15 minutes. Pour over bread, clam and eggs. Mix will and put into a 9 x 13 pan and bake for 30-40 minutes at 350°. For small batch use: 1 can clams, 1 loaf bread, 2 onions, 1-1/2 pounds butter, 2 tablespoons parsley, 1 teaspoon seasoning and 1 egg. By the way, the edges are the best!!! They get all crunchy and good.

Flattery should be used like perfume—smell and enjoy it, but don't swallow it.

Emerald Rice Bake

1/2 cup onions, chopped
1 tablespoon butter
2 cups cooked rice
1 can cream of mushroom soup
1 10-ounce package frozen chopped broccoli, thawed
1/2 cup cheddar cheese, shredded

Cook onions in butter just until tender. Stir in rice, soup and broccoli. Put into a shallow, buttered, 1-1/2 quart casserole. Top with cheese and bake at 350 for 30 minutes. You can use 3/4 pound fresh cooked broccoli.

Spaghetti Sauce

2 pounds ground beef
1 small onion, chopped
2 garlic cloves, crushed
1 large can tomatoes, chopped or diced
1 large can tomato sauce
1 small can tomato paste
1 tomato paste can water
mushrooms, optional
a few shakes of sweet basil
a shake or two of oregano
salt and pepper to taste
1 or 2 bay leaves

Brown meat and onions. Mix remaining ingredients and simmer to desired thickness. Don't forget to take out the bay leaves. This sauce is great for anything Italian. Spaghetti, lasagna, manicotti; just anything.

Alfredo Sauce

This is Bonnie Garvin's recipe and so very good.

1/4 cup butter
1/4 cup parmesan cheese, grated (freshly grated is the best)
salt and pepper to taste
1-1/2 teaspoons garlic powder
1-1/2 teaspoons parsley flakes
16 ounces sour cream

Melt butter slowly. Add cheese and seasonings. Simmer (do not boil). Add sour cream. Serve with shrimp, chicken and pasta.

Casseroles & Meat Pies

Chop Suey Casserole

This was Grandma Hazel's recipe.

Brown together:
2 pounds chop suey meat
1 medium onion, chopped

Add:
1 cup celery, chopped
1 can cream of mushroom soup
1 can chicken and rice soup
2 cups water, more if necessary
1 can mushrooms with juice
3/4 cup raw white rice
1 tablespoon soy sauce
pinch of salt

Mix together, put in baking dish. Bake at 325° for 2 hours. Stir last half hour and scatter almond slices on top. Another good addition to this is a can of sliced water chestnuts.

Best Chicken Casserole

2 cups cooked chicken, bite size
1 cup celery, diced
1 cup almonds, sliced
1 cup mayonnaise
1 can cream of chicken soup
1 pound crushed potato chips
1 cup cheddar cheese, grated

Mix chicken, celery and almonds. Mix mayonnaise and soup. Then add chicken. Put into casserole, cover with chips and top with cheese. Cover, bake at 350° for 40-45 minutes.

Chicken Casserole

This recipe came from Lila Carstensen.

4 whole chicken breasts, cooked, boned
2 cans cream of chicken or cream of mushroom soup
1/2 - 3/4 soup can of milk
1 package Pepperidge® Farm stuffing
1 cup water or chicken broth
1/2 cup margarine

Keep chicken in large pieces. Lay in bottom of casserole. Sprinkle with salt and pepper, mix soup and milk and pour over chicken. Combine stuffing, water and margarine, spread over top. A little chopped onion can be added to stuffing. Bake 1 hour at 350°. Can make a day in advance, but do not freeze. I like to add 1 can sliced water chestnuts on top of the chicken layer and I usually add some sliced almonds and apple to the dressing layer.

Reuben Casserole

This is one of several recipes Val Hartman brought to work. I've made this and it's very good.

2 cans mushroom soup
1-1/3 cups milk
1/2 cup onion, chopped
1 tablespoon mustard
2 16-ounce cans of sauerkraut, drained
1 8-ounce package of uncooked noodles
1-1/2 pounds Polish sausage or Kielbasa, cut in 1/2 inch pieces
2 cups swiss cheese, shredded
3/4 cup bread crumbs
2 tablespoons butter, melted

Combine first 4 ingredients and blend well. Spread sauerkraut in a greased 9 x 13 inch pan. Top with noodles, cover with soup mixture. Top with sausage and cheese. Mix breadcrumbs with butter and sprinkle over the top. Cover with foil and bake at 350° for 1 hour or till noodles are tender. Serves 8-10.

Cabbage Roll Casserole

Carol Morrison has made this for many large gatherings; so with a smile we call this 'wedding and funeral' food because the longer it rests the better it is.

1 cup raw rice
2 pounds raw hamburger
lots of onion, chopped
salt and pepper
1 large can chopped tomatoes
2 tablespoons vinegar
2 tablespoons brown sugar
cabbage, chopped

Mix together the rice, hamburger, onions, salt and pepper to taste. Combine the chopped tomatoes, vinegar and brown sugar to make the tomato mixture. Layer chopped cabbage, meat mixture and tomato mixture. End up layers with tomato mixture and cabbage. Bake at least 1-1/2 hours. Great!!! Tip: Gug used to freeze her cabbage because it cooked faster.

Tater Tot Casserole

This is a time honored casserole that I never made until 1995. I'm not sure why, but now I wonder why I waited so long. It's really good.

1 - 2 pounds ground beef
onion, chopped
1 can cream of chicken soup
1 can French cut green beans, drained
tater tots

Brown ground beef, add chopped onions, to taste. Add cream of chicken soup and mix well. Put in the bottom of a greased casserole dish. Layer green beans on top of meat. Arrange tater tots on top of beans and bake at 350° for about 30 minutes. I often add a little milk to the soup. It helps to keep everything more moist. Some people also line the casserole with tater tots before layering the other ingredients.

Zucchini Casserole

1 pound pork sausage
1 cup onions, chopped
1 cup green pepper, chopped
1/2 cup chicken broth
1 can cream of chicken soup
5 cups zucchini, chopped
1 teaspoon salt
1/8 teaspoon pepper
1/4 teaspoon garlic powder
3 cups rice, cooked
grated cheese

Brown and drain pork sausage, add the onion and green pepper and cook until onions are tender. Add chicken broth and soup. Add zucchini, salt, pepper and garlic and cook about 10 minutes, add rice. Pour into casserole and sprinkle with grated cheese. Bake till hot at 350°, season with salt, pepper, and garlic powder.

Potato Casserole

1 pound bag frozen hash brown potatoes, thawed
salt and pepper to taste
1 can cream of chicken soup
1 cup cheddar cheese, shredded
1/4 cup onion, chopped
1/2 - 1 cup sour cream
1/4 cup butter, melted
1 cup corn flakes or potato chips, crushed

Mix all ingredients together, except the butter and cornflakes or potato chips, and put into a casserole. Mix together the melted butter and corn flakes or potato chips and place on top of the casserole. Bake at 350° for 40 minutes uncovered.

Spaket Of Corned Beef

Grandma Hazel's Recipe

1 package creamettes
1 12-ounce can corned beef
1/4 pound American cheese, cubed
1 can cream of chicken soup
1 cup milk
1/4 cup onion, chopped
1/2 cup buttered crumbs

Mix all together except crumbs. Sprinkle crumbs on top and bake at 375° for 1 hour.

Pasty Pie (or Pasties)

Marty Seid gave me this crust recipe and it's perfect for pasties. It pulls and stretches well.

1 cup shortening
1 cup boiling water
1/2 teaspoon salt
3-1/2 cups flour

chuck roast, coarsely ground
potatoes, chopped or ground
carrots, chopped or ground
onion, chopped or ground
rutabaga, chopped or ground
salt and pepper

Melt shortening in boiling water in mixing bowl. Mix in salt and flour and set aside. When meat and vegetables are ready, mix together. Divide dough into 2 crusts for pasty pie. Fill bottom crust with meat and vegetable mixture. Season to taste with salt and pepper. Cover with top crust. Put slashes in top and brush with egg wash. Bake at 350° for 1 hour.

Note: For pasties, divide dough into 12. Roll out the 12 small rounds of dough, put some of the filling on one side and fold the crust over, sealing the edges. (Use the desired amount of meat and vegetables, I use a good 1/2 cup mixture per pasty.) Bake at 350° for 25-30 minutes.

Pork Pie

This is Bonnie Harris' recipe. She's gone from us now, but I think of her often, especially at the New Year when I make her pork pie.

> pie crust
> 8 pounds ground pork
> 3 pounds potatoes, boiled, and just mashed, no milk, no nothing
> 1/2 bag onions, minced
> salt
> pepper
> sage
> poultry seasoning
> Sometimes I use a little allspice and ginger
> pastry for a double crust pie

Mix all ingredients, season to taste. You should figure about 2 pounds meat to a pie. Put this mixture into pie crust and cover with top crush. Brush with beaten egg. Bake at 350° for an hour.

Dear God,
Let me remember, when I was young
The games I played, the songs I sung.
The joys I savored, the hurts I hid
The foolish things I said and did.

Have lived so long in this grown-up land
That a child is hard to understand.
O God, let me go back, and fancy see
The heart of the child I used to be,
So the heart of my child will be clear to me.

Chicken Dishes

Chicken Enchiladas

> 1 can tomato sauce
> 1 small can green chilies
> 1 onion, chopped
> corn tortillas
> chicken, cooked and diced
> cheddar cheese, shredded
> 1 small container of sour cream

Mix tomato sauce, chilies and onion in a sauce pan. Spread some of sauce in the bottom of a 7 x 11 cake pan. Dip one side of corn tortilla in sauce and lay sauce side up on counter. Fill with chicken and cover with shredded cheddar cheese. Roll up, and put into pan. Continue until pan is full. Add sour cream to remaining sauce, pour over enchiladas, and cover with more cheese. Bake till cheese is completely melted.

Grandma Eva's Fried Chicken

> flour
> cornflake crumbs (about twice as much as the flour)
> salt and pepper, to taste
> 1 cut up chicken, dividing legs and thighs and breasts and wings
> 1-1/2 cups milk
> oil

Combine the flour, cornflakes crumbs, salt and pepper. Dip chicken pieces in milk, then shake in a bag containing the cornflake mixture. Fry until browned in about 1/2 inch oil, then put in a baking dish with a rack and bake for an hour or until chicken is tender. Of course you understand, Grandma Eva fried hers in lard and didn't use a rack in baking. I'm sure hers was better; this might be just a little healthier.

Chicken And Gleasons

This is another of Grandma Eva's specialties. It was a Sunday staple. Gleasons are a French dumpling, and oh, so good.

Cover chicken pieces with water in a large pot or a roasting pan and simmer on stove top until chicken is very tender. Remove from broth and cool until you can take the meat off the bones. In the meantime, I add a little chicken bouillon or soup base (a couple of tablespoons). You can thicken this a little with flour and water or a package of chicken gravy mix. Don't thicken too much, though, as the gleasons will do that when you add them to the chicken. Put chicken meat back into the pot and make gleasons. The recipe is in the bread section (page 128). Put them into the chicken to cook about 30 minutes before you serve. Serve with mashed potatoes and Grandma Eva's salad. MMMM.

Creamed Chicken And Biscuits

Mom's was the best, but this is mine.

1 chicken, cut up
1 onion, chopped
2 - 3 cups water or chicken broth
1/2 cup butter
1/2 cup flour
about 1 cup broth used in cooking chicken
1 cup whole milk
salt and pepper
garlic
paprika
Worcestershire sauce
olives, optional

Cook chicken and onion in water or broth. Remove chicken when it is very tender, reserving broth. Cool until you can handle it easily. To make the cream sauce, stir together the butter and flour in a pan. Add broth and milk slowly, stirring until thick. Season with salt, pepper, garlic, paprika and a little Worcestershire sauce. If it's too thick, add a little more broth.

Remove the chicken from the bones, break it up in bite size pieces and put into the cream sauce. Mom always added olives to this. Simmer for about 30 minutes, stirring to avoid sticking. Serve with rice and or biscuits (found in the bread section-page 118).

Chicken And Dumplings

chicken, about 3 pounds, cut up
8 cups chicken stock
1 large onion, chopped
about 1 cup celery, chopped
salt and pepper, to taste
garlic salt, to taste
2 bay leaves
1 can cream of celery soup
1 can cream of chicken soup

Simmer the chicken in the stock with the onion, celery and seasoning. When the chicken is tender, remove and cool it enough to remove the bones. Cut into bite size pieces and return to the pot. Add the soup and cook gently for another 20 or 30 minutes. If you like it a little thicker, just add a little flour and water. I serve this with dumplings made with biscuit mix or with rice and biscuits.

Wouldn't it be nice if we could find other things as easily as we find fault?

Parmesan Chicken

This is a variation of fried chicken and it has a wonderful flavor.

chicken
butter
flour
parmesan cheese, grated

Prepare chicken as you would for fried chicken, dip it in butter and shake in a mixture of flour and parmesan cheese. About half as much cheese as flour. Place in a buttered pan and drizzle with butter. Bake at 350° for about an hour. Turn about half way through baking.

Chicken Cordon Bleu

This is a very good meal for company.

chicken breasts, boneless
swiss cheese, sliced
ham, sliced
flour
eggs, beaten
bread crumbs
oil

Flatten boneless chicken breasts slightly between two sheets of wax paper. On inner side, lay 1 slice of swiss cheese and 1 slice of ham in center of breast. Roll it up and fasten with a toothpick. Roll breast in flour, then in beaten eggs, and then in bread crumbs. Brown in oil and bake at 350° for 45 minutes to an hour. Serve with mushroom sauce.

Mushroom Sauce:

1 chicken bouillon cube
2/3 cup boiling water
2 tablespoons butter
2 tablespoons flour
2 teaspoons Worcestershire sauce
1 small can mushrooms, drained, chopped finely
1/2 cup sour cream

Dissolve chicken bouillon in boiling water. In small pan melt butter and blend in flour. Add bouillon all at once. Mix well, stirring constantly until thickened. Stir in Worcestershire sauce, mushrooms and sour cream. Serve hot.

Breakfast Dishes & Quiche

Potato Onion Breakfast Bake

We had this in Ireland. It's easy and very good.

> 3 cups potatoes, medium diced
> 3 tablespoons olive oil
> 1 cup onion, diced
> 10 large eggs, whipped
> salt and pepper

Cook, in an oven-safe deep pan, the potatoes in the olive oil. When they've begun to soften, cover with the onion. Cook together until soft.

Cover with the eggs, salt and pepper well. Bake at 350° until eggs are set. Broil top for a minute or two. Turn out onto a plate. This is good for a lunch as well if served with a salad.

Karen's Sausage Gravy

Karen is specific about the brands she uses for this, so here it is.

> 1 package McCormick® sausage gravy mix, (makes 2 cups)
> 2% milk or chicken broth
> pepper
> 1/2 tube Jimmy Dean® spicy sausage, browned

Mix the gravy mix with the milk or chicken broth, season with lots of pepper and add to the sausage. Great with biscuits.

Overnight Omelet

> crustless bread
> 8 - 12 ounces cheese of your choice, shredded
> 12 eggs
> 1 cup milk
> ham, cooked bacon or sausage

Butter a 9 x 13 pan and line the bottom with bread. Sprinkle with cheese (I prefer cheddar). Beat the eggs with milk and pour over the cheese. Top with meat of your choice and let set overnight in the refrigerator. Bake at 375° for 40-50 minutes. Makes 12 large servings.

Easter Pie

This was Judy McDonough's specialty and is absolutely super!

1 8 inch pie shell, unbaked
8 eggs, beaten
1/2 cup parmesan cheese, grated
1/2 teaspoon salt
1/4 teaspoon white pepper
1/4 teaspoon baking powder

Mix the last 5 ingredients well and pour into crust. Bake at 350° for 30 minutes, until golden brown.

Gruyere Quiche

To roast tomatoes:

Cut, in half, seed and arrange 10 tomatoes on a baking sheet. Drizzle with olive oil, sprinkle with garlic powder and herbs de province and salt. Bake at 250° for 1-1/2 to 2 hours. Do not turn off oven. When done, remove from oven and set aside.

Ingredients:
1 white onion, finely chopped
1/2 pound bacon, diced
8 eggs
2 cups créme fraiche or heavy cream
2 tablespoons tomato puree or sauce
1 tablespoon chives, chopped
1 cup Gruyere cheese, shredded

Sauté onions in 1 tablespoon olive oil for 3-5 minutes. Remove to a paper towel and crisp the bacon in the same pan. Drain on paper towels. Whisk the eggs, créme fraiche and tomato puree. Stir in chives, bacon and onions.

Arrange tomato halves in a round casserole dish. Top with the cheese. Pour in the egg mixture. Tomatoes will probably float to the top during baking. Bake at 350° for 50-60 minutes or until golden brown and eggs are set. This is wonderful.

Broccoli Quiche With Potato Crust

> 2 cups potatoes, grated
> 3/4 teaspoon salt
> 1 egg
> 1/3 cup onion, grated

Salt potatoes and let them set for about 15 minutes. Squeeze out moisture. Mix with egg and onion. Press into a large greased pie plate. Make sure to press it up the sides as well. Bake at 400° for 30-40 minutes. You can spray the crust with a butter spray and turn on the broiler for a minute or so at the end. This will make it crisp.

> Filling ingredients:
> 2 10-ounce boxes frozen chopped broccoli, thawed and drained
> 3 tablespoons butter
> 1 cup onion, finely chopped
> 1 - 2 cloves minced garlic
> 1 teaspoon salt
> 1/4 teaspoon pepper
> 1/2 teaspoon dry basil
> 1/2 teaspoon thyme
> 2 tablespoons chives, chopped
> 3 - 4 tablespoons parmesan cheese, grated
> 1-3/4 cups Gruyere cheese, grated or shredded
> 1/2 cup milk or cream
> 4 eggs

Sauté broccoli in butter with onion and garlic for about 5 minutes, until gently browned. Add the spices and stir together. Layer the crust with half the cheese, the broccoli mixture and the rest of the cheese. Mix the milk or cream and the eggs together, then pour over the cheese. Bake at 350° for 35-40 minutes. It may sound like a lot of work, but it really goes together fast. Serve warm or at room temp.

Breads, Rolls, Coffee Cakes & Muffins

Breads, Rolls, Coffee Cakes & Muffins

Whole Wheat Bread

3 cups white flour
3 cups whole wheat flour
1/4 cup firmly packed brown sugar
2 packages active dry yeast
1 tablespoon salt
1/4 cup butter or margarine (I use bacon fat)
1 cup milk
1 cup water
3 tablespoons cracked wheat (I use wheat germ)

Combine flours in a separate bowl. In mixing bowl, measure 2 cups flour, stir in sugar, yeast and salt. In saucepan, heat butter, milk and water until butter melts (120 - 130 degrees). Gradually add milk mixture to flour mixture, beat at low until smooth, about 2 minutes. Add 1/2 - 3/4 cup flour or enough to make thick batter, beat for 5 minutes longer, at high speed. Stir in as much of the remaining flour as possible with a wooden spoon to make a soft dough. Place on lightly floured surface and knead in any remaining flour. Continue kneading until smooth and elastic, about 10 minutes. Place in greased bowl, cover, set to rise in a warm place until doubled, about 1-1/2 hours. Punch down and divide in half. Grease 2 loaf pans, sprinkle each with cracked wheat. Shape dough into loaves, set aside in warm place to rise until reaching top of pans, about 1 hour. Preheat oven to 375°. Lightly brush tops of loaves with water and sprinkle with 1 tablespoon cracked wheat. Bake 35-40 minutes. Remove from pans and cool on wire racks.

Beer Bread

3 cups self rising flour
3 tablespoons sugar
1 bottle beer, room temperature

Mix all together by hand. Grease 1 loaf pan, pour mixture in. Bake at 350° for 1 hour.

Aunt Maxine's White Bread

This is a wonderful recipe that came from Shirley Stanley's Aunt Maxine.

1/2 cup Crisco®
4 cups water
2 tablespoons salt
1/2 cup sugar
4 eggs, beaten
1/4 cup yeast or 4 packages
10 cups flour

Melt shortening in hot water. Add salt, sugar and beaten eggs. Then add yeast. Stir in about 7 cups flour. Batter will be quite stiff (I use a mixer for this). Put remaining 3 cups flour on the counter, make a well and fill with batter. Knead together. Put into large greased bowl and let rise in a warm place until doubled. Punch down and let rise again. When doubled again, separate dough into 5 loaves and put into pan. Let rise once more until doubled. Bake at 375° for about 30 minutes, until golden brown.

Sweet Rye Bread

1 cup dark Karo® syrup
1 cup brown sugar
2 packages (4-1/2 teaspoons) dry yeast
1/2 cup warm water
4 cups rye flour
9 - 10 cups white flour
2 tablespoons salt
5 tablespoons margarine, melted in 4 cups hot water

Combine the Karo® syrup and brown sugar, heat and let cool to room temperature. Put the yeast into the 1/2 cup warm water. Mix together the rye flour and white flour and add salt. In a mixer bowl, put 3 cups of the flour mixture. Add the 4 cups water and margarine mixture and the yeast. Mix until well blended and then gradually add the remaining flour. For this step, change to a dough hook. If the dough becomes too thick for the mixer, put the rest of the flour onto a board and mix and knead by hand a good 5 to 10 minutes. Put in a large greased bowl. Cover and let rise in a warm place until doubled, about 2 hours. Punch down, divide into 6 portions. Shape and put into greased bread pans. Let rise again until it's about 1 inch above the top of the pan. Bake at 325° for 45-60 minutes.

Breads, Rolls, Coffee Cakes & Muffins

English Muffin Bread

This is another of Shirley and Wayne Stanley's recipes and it's one I make regularly. It makes the best toast ever and it is so easy.

> 5 cups flour, divided
> 4-1/2 teaspoons yeast or 2 packages
> 1 tablespoon sugar
> 2 teaspoons salt
> 1/4 teaspoon baking soda
> 2 cups warm skim milk, 120-130 degrees
> 1/2 cup warm water, 120-130 degrees
> 2 tablespoons cornmeal, divided

In mixing bowl, combine 2 cups flour, yeast, sugar, salt, and baking soda. Add warm milk and water. Beat on low for 30 seconds. Scrape sides of the bowl and beat on high for 3 minutes. Stir in remaining flour. Batter will be stiff. Do not knead this bread. Sprinkle bottoms of 2 greased pans with cornmeal. Divide the batter between the two pans, and sprinkle the rest of the cornmeal on the top. Let rise in a warm place until doubled, about 45 minutes. Bake at 375° for 35 minutes or until golden brown.

Multi-grain English Muffin Bread

Ruth Taylor preferred this variation and it is a good one.

> 1 package yeast
> 1-1/4 cups warm water
> 1/3 cup whole wheat flour
> 1/3 cup quick cooking oatmeal
> 1/3 cup wheat germ
> 1 tablespoon sugar
> 3/4 teaspoon salt
> 1/4 - 2 cups flour
> cornmeal, optional

Dissolve yeast in warm water. Add wheat flour, oatmeal, wheat germ, sugar and salt. Beat until smooth and add flour, enough to make a soft dough. Let rise in a greased bowl until doubled. Punch down and shape into a loaf. Put in a bread pan and let rise again until doubled. Bake at 400° for 25 to 30 minutes. Cornmeal can be sprinkled on top and bottom if desired.

Really Good And Easy White Bread

You will find the recipe for this bread in main meals under Reuben Loaf. Your house will smell wonderful and it won't last long at all.

3 - 3-1/2 cups flour
1 package quick rise yeast
1 tablespoon sugar
1 tablespoon butter, softened
1 teaspoon salt
1 cup warm water
1 egg white, beaten

Mix about 2-1/2 cups flour, yeast, sugar, butter and salt. Add water and mix to a soft dough. Flour a board with the rest of the flour and knead for about 4 minutes. Form into a loaf, I like it braided, and let rise until doubled, about 45 minutes. Brush with egg white and bake at 375° for about 35 minutes.

Zucchini Bread

Mix in bowl:
2 eggs, beaten
1 cup oil
2 cups brown sugar
2 cups zucchini, ground
2 teaspoons vanilla
1 teaspoon salt

Combine in separate bowl:
3 cups flour
1 teaspoon baking soda
1/4 teaspoon baking powder
1 tablespoon cinnamon, optional
1/2 cup nuts, chopped

Combine all these ingredients together and mix well. Pour into 2 greased pans. Bake at 375° for 50-60 minutes.

Breads, Rolls, Coffee Cakes & Muffins

Zucchini Bread II

3 eggs
2 cups sugar
1 cup oil
1 tablespoon vanilla
1 teaspoon salt
1 teaspoon baking soda
1/2 teaspoon baking powder
2 cups zucchini, ground
1 cup crushed pineapple, drained
3 cups flour
1 cup nuts, chopped

Beat eggs and add rest of ingredients as given. Pour into 2 greased pans. Bake at 350° for 50-60 minutes.

Apple Bread

1 cup sugar
1/2 cup shortening
2 eggs, beaten
1 teaspoon baking soda
1 tablespoon sour milk or buttermilk
2 cups flour
1/2 teaspoon salt
2 cups apples, coarsely chopped
1 teaspoon vanilla
1/2 cup nuts, chopped

Cream sugar, shortening and eggs. Add baking soda to buttermilk and stir well. Add to sugar mixture. Stir in flour and salt. Fold in apples, vanilla and nuts. Pour batter into 2 bread tins. Cover with topping.

Topping:
2 tablespoons margarine
1/2 teaspoon cinnamon
2 tablespoons sugar
2 tablespoons flour

Pour over batter, and bake at 350° for 45-50 minutes.

Cinnamon Quick Bread

This is from my friend and neighbor, Marty Seid. We spent many summer days eating this on my front porch. It's quick and very good.

1/2 cup oil
2 cups sugar
3 eggs
2 cups buttermilk
2 teaspoons baking soda dissolved in buttermilk
4 cups flour
1 teaspoon salt

Combine in order given.

Topping:
1 cup sugar
1/2 cup brown sugar
2 tablespoons cinnamon

Grease and flour 2 bread pans. Divide 1/2 of batter between the two pans. Then divide 1/2 of the topping and sprinkle over batter. Repeat with the rest of the batter, then the rest of the topping mixture. Swirl with a knife. Bake at 325° for 45-60 minutes. Cool 10 minutes in pans. Remove from pans and cool on rack.

Banana Bread

1 cup sugar
1 egg
1/3 cup shortening
3 large bananas, mashed
1 teaspoon salt
1/2 teaspoon baking soda
3 teaspoons baking powder
1 tablespoon sour milk
2 cups flour

Mix sugar, egg and shortening. Add bananas, salt, baking soda, baking powder and milk. Add flour last. Pour into greased loaf pan and bake at 350° for 1 hour.

Breads, Rolls, Coffee Cakes & Muffins

Gum Drop Bread

Mix in order given:

1 cup margarine
2 cups sugar
2 eggs
1 pound raisins
1 cup walnuts, chopped
1 pound gumdrops
1-1/2 cups applesauce
1 teaspoon vanilla
1 tablespoon hot water
1 teaspoon baking soda
4 cups flour
1 teaspoon cinnamon
1/4 teaspoon cloves, ground
1/4 teaspoon nutmeg
1/4 teaspoon salt

Pour into greased loaf pans. Bake at 350° for 1 hour.

Date Nut Loaf

This is Grandma Hazel's recipe and it's a favorite.

2 cups boiling water
1 pound dates (or raisins), chopped
2 teaspoons baking soda
1 teaspoon salt
2 cups sugar
1 cup shortening
2 eggs
4 cups flour
2 teaspoons vanilla
1/2 cup nuts, chopped

Pour boiling water over dates, baking soda and salt. Set aside to cool. Cream together the sugar, shortening and eggs. Add date mixture and then add flour, vanilla and nuts. Pour into greased loaf pan and bake at 350° for 1 hour. I make this bread in cans. It's a little different and very nice.

Sweet Rolls Or Doughnuts

1 cup milk
1/2 cup shortening
1/2 cup sugar
1 teaspoon salt
2 eggs
2 packages dry yeast dissolved in 1/2 cup warm water
4 cups or more flour to make a soft dough

Scald milk, add shortening, sugar and salt. Cool a little and add eggs, yeast and beat in flour, 1 cup at a time. Set in warm place to rise until doubled. Stir down and let rise again. Roll out on a floured board. Shape into buns, doughnuts, cinnamon rolls or whatever. Let rise and bake at 350° until browned, about 20 minutes. To make chocolate doughnuts, leave out 1/4 cup flour and add 1-1/2 squares melted chocolate and 1/4 teaspoon vanilla. Doughnuts can be deep fried.

Butterhorn Rolls

This wonderful little crescent shaped roll is to die for. I got it from Marty Seid's good friend Kathy Hogard.

3 cups flour
1 cup butter
3 tablespoons sugar
1 teaspoon salt
1 package yeast
1/2 cup warm milk
a pinch of sugar
3 eggs, well beaten

Combine flour, butter, 3 tablespoons sugar and salt, mix like pastry. Mix the yeast with the warm milk, add sugar and eggs, combine with pastry mixture, mixing well and chill overnight. Divide dough into 4 parts. Roll each into a circle and cut into 12 pie shaped pieces. Roll up like a crescent roll and let rise until double. Bake at 375° for 20 minutes or until golden brown. For a sweet treat, frost the rolls with a butter cream frosting. I usually make them with the frosting.

Breads, Rolls, Coffee Cakes & Muffins

Popovers

> 1 cup flour
> 1 egg, unbeaten
> 1 cup milk
> pinch of salt

Butter 12 muffin tins well and put them in a hot oven. Mix all the ingredients together and beat until well blended and smooth. When muffin tins are hissing hot, pour batter into them to 1/2 to 2/3 full. Bake at 450° to 475° for 30 to 40 minutes or until they are well popped over. If you like them dryer inside, poke them with a toothpick and leave them in the oven with the door ajar for about 30 minutes.

Brioche

These take time, but they're really worth it. I just love them!!

> 1 package yeast
> 1/2 cup warm water
> 2 teaspoons sugar
> 1-1/4 teaspoons salt
> 3 eggs
> 1/2 cup butter, room temperature
> 3-1/2 to 4 cups flour
> 1 egg yolk, beaten with 1 tablespoon milk

In a large bowl, blend yeast with warm water and sugar. Let stand until bubbly. Stir in salt and eggs. Cut butter into small pieces and add yeast mixture along with 3-1/3 cups of the flour. Stir with wooden spoon until flour is evenly moistened and dough holds together. Then shape into a ball and place on a floured board. Knead until smooth and velvety (about 5 minutes), adding flour as necessary to prevent sticking. Place dough in a greased bowl, and turn once to grease top. Cover with plastic wrap and let rise in a warm place until doubled, 1-2 hours. Turn dough onto lightly floured board. Knead to release air. Return to greased bowl. Cover with plastic wrap, refrigerate for 12-24 hours. Stir or knead dough on floured board to release air. Shape dough by dividing into 12 equal portions. To shape, pinch off about 1/6th of each portion. Roll the larger portions into a smooth ball, and place in well greased muffin tins. Poke a hole in the top of each roll. Roll each small portion into a tiny ball and place in the hole on the top of the rolls. Cover with plastic wrap and let rise until doubled, 1-2 hours. With a soft brush, paint the tops with the egg yolk mixture. Bake at 425° for about 20 minutes or until richly browned. Serve warm. MMMMMMMMMMMMM, they're great!

Angel Biscuits

5 cups flour
1 teaspoon baking soda
3 teaspoons baking powder
1/4 cup sugar
1 package yeast dissolved in 1/4 cup warm water
1 cup Crisco®
2 cups buttermilk

Mix everything together well. Place in covered bowl store in refrigerator for up to a week. Drop by tablespoons onto greased cookie sheet. Bake at 425° for about 15 minutes.

Garlic Cheese Biscuits
Yes, these are served at a well known seafood restaurant.

2 cups buttermilk baking mix (Bisquick®)
2/3 cup milk
1/2 cup cheddar cheese, shredded
1/4 cup butter, melted
1/2 teaspoon garlic powder

Combine baking mix, milk and cheese in mixing bowl. Mix until soft dough forms. Drop dough by spoonfuls into ungreased cookie sheet. Bake at 450° for 8-10 minutes or until golden. Mix butter and garlic powder and brush over warm biscuits before removing from cookie sheet.

Easy Monkey Bread

3/4 cup sugar
1 teaspoon cinnamon
4 tubes buttermilk biscuits
1/2 cup margarine
1 cup brown sugar
1 teaspoon cinnamon

Put sugar and cinnamon in a bag. Cut biscuits in quarters and shake in the bag until coated. Place into greased bundt pan. (Can add a few chopped nuts as you layer.) Bring margarine, brown sugar and cinnamon to a boil and pour over biscuits. Bake at 350° for 35-40 minutes. Invert pan on serving plate and enjoy.

Breads, Rolls, Coffee Cakes & Muffins

Overnight Dough

This can be used for coffee cake, rolls or tea cakes.

5 cups flour
3/4 cup shortening
1/2 cup sugar
1/2 tablespoon salt
2 cups cold milk
2 eggs
1 package yeast

Mix half of the flour, shortening, sugar and salt like pie crust. Add milk, eggs and yeast. Add the rest of the flour and mix well. Refrigerate dough overnight.

Shout or scream… I'll bet you won't be heard.
But whisper, sister… they'll not miss a word.

Mouthwatering Quick Cinnamon Rolls

This is a great one from Julie.

1 loaf of frozen bread dough, thawed
1/4 cup margarine
1 teaspoon cinnamon
1/4 cup brown sugar
chopped nuts, if desired
1/4 cup butter
1 tablespoon Karo® syrup
1/2 cup brown sugar

Roll out bread dough. Melt margarine, (I don't melt it all the way). Brush over bread dough. Sprinkle with a mixture of the cinnamon, 1/4 cup brown sugar and the chopped nuts. Roll up from the long side, and cut into 10 pieces.

Bring just to a boil, the butter, Karo® syrup and the 1/2 cup brown sugar. Pour this mixture into a pie tin and place rolls on top. Let rise and bake at 375° for about 20 minutes.

Grandma Hansen's Famous Coffee Cake

1-1/4 cups milk
1 package yeast
1/2 teaspoon sugar
1/2 cup warm water (about 130 degrees)
3/4 stick butter, soft
1/2 cup sugar
2 eggs
2 teaspoons vanilla
1/4 teaspoon salt
2 teaspoons ground cardamom
2 cups flour

Scald milk. Dissolve yeast and 1/2 teaspoon sugar in warm water, set aside. In mixer, cream together butter and 1/2 cup sugar. Add eggs and mix until well combined. Add vanilla and salt. Add yeast mixture, cardamom, milk and 2 cups flour. Continue to add flour 1 cup at a time until dough is very thick. Cover and let rise in a warm place until doubled, about 1 hour. Flour board and turn dough out onto board, divide dough into 3 sections. Divide each section into 3 and braid loosely. "Hit the kids in the face with the braid." Put in a pie pan (curved) let double in size again, another hour. Bake at 350° for about 30 minutes. Top with the following glaze while still warm.

Note: Grandma really did slap us lightly in the face with the dough. I think we lined up to run through the kitchen when she was baking this.

Sourdough Starter

1 package dry yeast
2 tablespoons sugar or honey
2 cups warm water
1/3 cup nonfat dry milk
2 cups flour

In large non-metal container, dissolve yeast and sugar in water. Let stand until foamy, 5-10 minutes. With wooden spoon, stir in dry milk and flour. Small lumps in batter will dissolve with fermentation process. Cover container with 2-3 layers of cheesecloth. Secure with a rubber band. Set in warm place free from drafts. Stir mixture several times a day. Let stand 3 to 5 days until starter has a pleasant sour aroma and is full of bubbles. Note: If starter turns pink or orange, mixture must be thrown out and start over.

Breads, Rolls, Coffee Cakes & Muffins

Herman Coffee Cake

2 cups sourdough starter
2 cups flour
1 cup sugar
2/3 cup oil
2 eggs
2 teaspoons baking powder
1/2 teaspoon baking soda
1/2 teaspoon salt
1/2 teaspoon cinnamon

Mix well and pour into greased 9 x 13 pan.

Topping:
1 tablespoon flour
2 teaspoons cinnamon
1 cup brown sugar
1/2 cup melted margarine

Mix dry ingredients and sprinkle over cake batter. Drizzle margarine over the top and cut through batter with a knife. Bake at 350° for 35-40 minutes. Glaze with powdered sugar glaze or 1 stick margarine, 1/2 cup brown sugar and 1/2 cup milk boiled together for 5 minutes. This is very rich.

Glaze

3/4 pound powdered sugar
2 tablespoons butter, melted
milk

Combine powdered sugar and butter, add enough milk to make desired consistancy

Glaze II
This is another very good glaze for Herman Coffee Cake.

1 cup maple syrup
1/4 cup butter

Boil for 5 minutes and pour over cake.

Maple Nut Coffee Twist

This is everyone's favorite.

1 package hot roll mix
3 tablespoons sugar
3/4 cup hot tap water
1 teaspoon maple flavoring
1 egg
1/2 cup sugar
1/3 cup walnuts, chopped
1 teaspoon cinnamon
1 teaspoon maple flavoring
6 tablespoons margarine, melted
1-1/2 cups powdered sugar
2 - 3 tablespoons milk
1/4 teaspoon maple flavoring
2 tablespoons margarine, softened

Grease 12 inch pizza pan. Combine hot roll mix with 3 tablespoons sugar. Stir in water, 1 teaspoon maple flavoring and egg. Mix until a ball forms. Knead on floured surface 2-3 minutes, until no longer sticky. Let rise in a greased bowl until doubled, 30-45 minutes. Combine 1/2 cup sugar, walnuts, cinnamon and 1 teaspoon maple flavoring and mix well. Divide dough into 3 equal balls. Roll one ball to fit pan. Brush with melted butter and sprinkle with 1/3 of the cinnamon mixture. Repeat with other two balls, ending with filling. Use a glass to mark a center (about a 2 inch center). Do Not cut through the dough with the glass. From the outside edge to the glass, cut 16 pie shaped portions. Twist each of the 3 layered wedges 5 times. Let rise in a warm place until doubled, about 30 minutes. Bake at 375° for about 20 minutes until golden.

Combine powdered sugar, milk, maple flavoring and margarine until smooth. Drizzle over warm coffee cake.

Sympathy is two hearts tugging at one load.

Breads, Rolls, Coffee Cakes & Muffins

Apple Cream Coffee Cake

Gail Guertin brought this to school for my birthday. It was wonderful.

1/2 cup nuts, chopped
2 teaspoons cinnamon
1-1/2 cups sugar
1/2 cup butter
2 eggs
1 teaspoon vanilla
2 cups flour
1 teaspoon baking powder
1/2 teaspoon salt
1 teaspoon baking soda
1 cup sour cream
Apples, sliced

In a small bowl, mix nuts, cinnamon and 1/2 cup sugar. Grease angel food cake pan. Beat butter until creamy and add 1 cup sugar. Add eggs one at a time and then vanilla. Mix flour with baking powder, salt and baking soda. Beat into batter alternately with the sour cream. Spread half of the batter in cake pan. Top it with sliced apples and half the sugar mixture. Then layer on the rest of the batter and the rest of the sugar mixture. Bake at 375° for 40 minutes. Remove from the oven and let stand on wire rack for about 30 minutes. Lift out cake on base of pan and let it continue to cool on rack. Very good.

Nutty Coffee Cake

Sister Rita Mae gave us this recipe.

2 packages frozen roll dough or 1-1/2 loaves frozen bread dough cut into 24 pieces
1/2 cup nuts, chopped
1 package vanilla pudding (cooked style)
1/2 cup brown sugar
1 stick margarine

Grease bundt pan. Place rolls in pan with the nuts. Combine pudding and brown sugar. Sprinkle over rolls. Melt margarine and drizzle over rolls. Cover with a towel and let stand overnight. Bake at 350° for 30 minutes. If you use bread dough, thaw only enough to cut into pieces. This is great for a holiday brunch.

Sour Cream Coffee Cake

Mix together for topping:
3/4 cup sugar
1 teaspoon cinnamon
1/2 cup nuts, chopped

Batter:
1/2 cup margarine
1 cup sugar
2 eggs
2 cups flour
1/2 teaspoon baking powder
1/2 teaspoon baking soda
1/2 teaspoon salt
1 cup sour cream

Cream margarine and sugar and add eggs one at a time. Beat well. Add flour, baking powder, baking soda and salt alternately with sour cream. Pour 1/2 of the batter into a 9 inch square cake pan. Sprinkle with 1/2 of the topping. Cover with the rest of the batter and sprinkle with the rest of the topping. Bake at 350° for about 35 minutes.

Honey Bun Coffee Cake

1 yellow cake mix
4 eggs
3/4 cup oil
1 cup sour cream

Mix together and put into a greased 9 x 13 pan.

1/3 cup good honey
1/3 cup brown sugar
1 tablespoon cinnamon
1/2 cup chopped nuts

Drizzle honey over batter. Combine brown sugar, cinnamon and nuts and sprinkle over honey. Swirl this with a knife to gently blend. Bake at 350° for 35-40 minutes. Make a glaze of 2 cups powdered sugar, 1/3 cup milk, and 1 teaspoon vanilla. Top the cake while it's hot.

Breads, Rolls, Coffee Cakes & Muffins

A rule of thumb for making good muffins is to mix the batter only until moistened. Do not over mix. It makes them tough.

Berry Cream Muffins

This is from my dear friend Marta, the blueberry picker.

4 cups flour
2 cups sugar
2 teaspoons baking powder
1 teaspoon baking soda
1 teaspoon salt
3 cups blueberries
4 eggs
2 cups sour cream
1 cup oil
1 teaspoon vanilla

Combine dry ingredients. Add berries, mixing gently. Combine eggs, sour cream, oil and vanilla. Stir into dry ingredients until just moist. Fill greased muffins 2/3 - 3/4 full. Bake 400° for about 15 minutes. Makes 3 dozen muffins.

Corn Muffins

1 egg
2/3 cup milk
1/3 cup melted margarine
1 cup flour
3/4 cup cornmeal
2 - 4 tablespoons sugar
1 teaspoon salt

Grease 12 muffin tins. Beat egg, milk and margarine together, then add rest of ingredients. Mix only until moist. Spoon into cups and bake at 400° for 20 minutes. Serve warm, dripping with butter.

Oatmeal Muffins

This recipe came from Lila Carstensen, a wonderful cook.

> 1 cup buttermilk
> 1 cup quick oatmeal
> 1/2 cup brown sugar
> 1 egg
> 1/2 cup Crisco® or margarine
> 1 cup flour
> 1/2 teaspoon salt
> 1 teaspoon baking powder
> 1/2 teaspoon baking soda

Pour buttermilk over oatmeal and let stand for 1 hour. Add rest of ingredients and mix just until blended. Grease 12 muffin tins and fill 2/3 full. Bake at 350° for 20 minutes.

Banana Muffins

When we went to Jamaica, the chef at our hotel made wonderful muffins each morning. At the end of our visit, he wrote his recipe out for me to take home. I was very grateful because he didn't usually give his recipes to people. I really enjoyed the way he wrote it, and the Jamaican influence, so I wanted to share it with you.

½ lbs Sugar ½ lbs. butter 2 tea Spoon Lime Juice
5 Eggs 1 Pint Milk 1 knife Point of Cinnamon 1 Tea Spoon
Vanilla. 1 lbs flour ½tea of baking Powder
and if you care for Rum or
brandy

Breads, Rolls, Coffee Cakes & Muffins

Grandma Hansen's Crepes
"All in Abouts"

> 2 - 3 eggs
> 2 tablespoons sugar
> 2 tablespoons oil or melted butter
> about 1 cup flour
> about 1-3/4 cups milk (no less)
> dash of salt

With mixer or whisk, beat well, but not frothy. Pour a little in a greased frying pan and tip pan just until bottom is coated. The thinner the better. Brown on one side and then flip and repeat. THEY'RE WONDERFUL!!!

Pancakes

> 2 cups buttermilk
> 2 eggs
> 2 tablespoons sugar
> 2 tablespoons oil
> 2 teaspoons baking soda
> 1 teaspoon salt
> 2 cups flour

Blend all ingredients in mixer. Fry on oiled griddle until golden on both sides. Serves 6.

German Potato Pancakes

> 1/3 cup flour
> 3 well beaten eggs
> 3 cups potatoes, coarsely grated
> 1 small onion, grated
> 2 teaspoons salt

Mix together with spoon and drop by spoonfuls onto buttered griddle or frying pan. Fry until brown and crispy on both sides. This is not a thin pancake.

Noodles And Gleasons

Grandma Eva made these most Sundays, gleasons are a French dumpling.

3 - 4 cups flour
1 egg
3/4 cup water
salt

Make a trench with the 3 or 4 cups flour and pour in a mixture the egg, water and salt. Mix with a fork, bringing the flour into the center. Add only enough flour so that you can handle the dough easily. Don't add too much flour. Roll out on board and cut into noodles or gleasons. Gleasons are more a square shape. Drop them in boiling soup or in simmering chicken and gravy.

Cakes &
Icings

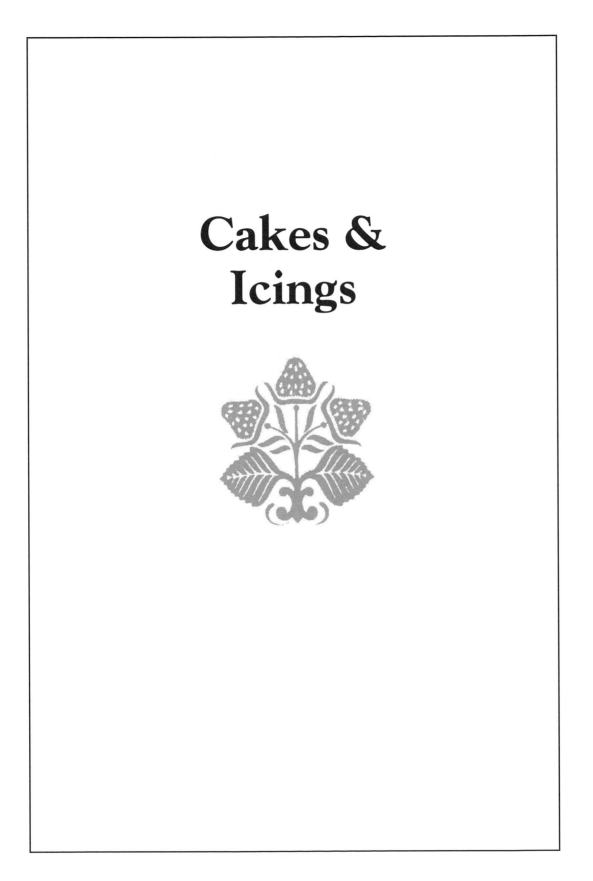

Chocolate Cake

1/2 cup shortening
1-1/2 cups sugar
1/2 cup cocoa
2 eggs
1/2 cup milk
2 teaspoons baking soda
a pinch of salt
2 cups flour
1 tablespoon vanilla
1 cup boiling water

Mix all ingredients except water, then add water real fast and mix well. Pour into 9 x 13 pan. Bake at 350° for about 30 minutes.

Chocolate Sheet Cake

1-1/4 cups margarine
1/2 cup cocoa
1 cup water
2 cups flour
1-1/2 cups brown sugar, firmly packed
1 teaspoon baking soda
1 teaspoon cinnamon
1/2 teaspoon salt
1 14-ounce can sweetened condensed milk
2 eggs
1 teaspoon vanilla
1 cup powdered sugar
1 cup nuts, chopped

Melt 1 cup margarine, stir in 1/4 cup cocoa, then the water. Bring to a boil, then remove from heat. Combine flour, brown sugar, baking soda, cinnamon and salt. Add cocoa mixture and beat well. Stir in 1/3 milk, eggs, and vanilla. Pour into a greased jelly roll pan and bake at 350° for 15 minutes. In saucepan, melt rest of margarine (1/4 cup), stir in the remaining 1/4 cup cocoa and remaining milk. Stir in powdered sugar and nuts. Spread on warm cake.

Deep Dark Chocolate Cake
You could die for this cake.

1-3/4 cups flour
2 cups sugar
3/4 cup cocoa
1-1/2 teaspoons baking soda
1-1/2 teaspoons baking powder
1 teaspoon salt
2 eggs
1/2 cup oil
1 cup milk
2 teaspoons vanilla
2 cups boiling water

Combine first 6 ingredients, add the eggs, oil, milk and vanilla and beat for 2 minutes. Stir in boiling water. Put into greased 9 x 13 pan. Bake at 350° for 35-40 minutes.

If you see any duplications in this book, it's because they're really good, and you really should try them...

Salad Dressing Cake

1-1/2 cups salad dressing
1-1/2 cups sugar
1 teaspoon vanilla
3 cups flour
3/4 cup cocoa
1-1/2 teaspoons baking soda
a dash of salt
1 cup cold water

Combine dressing, sugar and vanilla. Add dry ingredients alternately with water. Pour into greased 9 x 13 pan. Bake at 350° for 30-35 minutes. Cool and frost.

Nellie's Red Velvet Cake

My niece Katie says Nellie Smith makes the best Red Velvet Cake ever.

1 cup buttermilk
1 teaspoon white vinegar
2-1/2 cups flour
1-1/2 cups sugar
1 tablespoon baking soda
1 teaspoon cocoa
1-1/2 cups oil
2 eggs
1 tablespoon vanilla
1 bottle red food coloring

Mix buttermilk and vinegar together. Add all other ingredients at once. Put into 3 - 8 inch round cake pans and bake at 350° for 30 minutes. Frost with the following frosting:

Frosting:
1 box (1 pound) confectioner sugar
1 8-ounce package cream cheese
1 stick margarine
1 teaspoon vanilla
1 cup pecans, chopped, optional

Mix together and frost. Mmmm.

Joyce's Turtle Cake

1 German chocolate cake mix (regular chocolate cake is fine)
1 can sweetened condensed milk
1 jar caramel sauce
1 container Cool Whip®
toffee chips

Make cake mix as directed, bake. Poke holes in the cake with the end of a wooden spoon. Pour the condensed milk over the cake and then pour the caramel sauce over. Cool and refrigerate. Frost with Cool Whip® and top with toffee chips.

Texas Sheet Cake

2 cups flour
2 cups sugar
1/2 teaspoon salt
1 teaspoon cinnamon
2 sticks margarine
1 cup water
3 heaping tablespoons cocoa
2 well beaten eggs
1 teaspoon baking soda
1/2 cup buttermilk
1/2 teaspoon vanilla

Sift flour, sugar, salt and cinnamon together. In a saucepan, combine margarine, water and cocoa. Bring to a boil and pour over the flour mixture. In another bowl, put eggs, baking soda, buttermilk and vanilla. Add to above mixture and mix well. Bake in a greased jelly roll pan at 350° for 20 minutes.

Turtle Cake

1 German chocolate cake mix
3/4 cup margarine
1/2 cup evaporated milk
1 package caramels
1 cup chocolate chips
1 cup pecans
Cool Whip®

Mix cake according to directions. Pour half of batter into a greased 9 x 13 pan. Bake 15 minutes at 350°. While it's baking, mix margarine, milk and caramels. Blend until melted over low heat. Pour over cake, spread chips over this, then sprinkle on pecans. Top with remaining cake batter. Bake 20 minutes more. Serve with Cool Whip®.

Chocolate Date Cake

This rich moist cake is another of Grandma Hazel's recipes.

Combine and let stand:

> 1 cup hot water
> 1 cup cut-up dates
> 1 teaspoon baking soda

Cream:

> 3/4 cup shortening
> 1 cup sugar
> 2 eggs
> 2 squares bitter chocolate, melted

Add:

> 1-1/3 cups flour
> 1/2 teaspoon baking powder

Stir in date mixture and bake in 7 x 11 pan. Bake at 350° for 35 minutes.

Top with:

> 3/4 cup chocolate chips
> 1/2 cup chopped walnuts

Chocolate Sundae Cake

> 1 cup brown sugar
> 1/2 cup cocoa
> 2 cups water
> 2 cups mini marshmallows
> 1 package devils food cake mix
> 1 cup pecans, chopped

Combine sugar, cocoa and water. Mix well. Pour into 9 x 13 pan. Place marshmallows evenly on top. Mix cake according to directions and pour into pan. Top with nuts. Bake at 350° for 50 minutes.

Upside Down Fruit Cake

1 cup mini marshmallows
2-1/2 cups flour
1-1/2 cups sugar
1/2 cup shortening
3 teaspoons baking powder
1 cup milk
1 teaspoon vanilla
3 eggs
2 cups berries, crushed
1 package Jello®, same flavor

Grease bottom only of a 9 x 13 pan. Sprinkle marshmallows on bottom. Blend on low, flour, sugar, shortening, baking powder, milk, vanilla and eggs. Beat 3 minutes at medium. Pour batter over marshmallows. Mix berries with Jello®, spoon evenly over batter. Bake until golden brown at 350° for about 45 minutes. When toothpick inserted in middle comes out clean.

One should learn to disagree without becoming disagreeable.

Better Than Sex Cake

1 yellow cake mix
1 15-1/2 ounce can crushed pineapple
1 cup brown sugar
1 large vanilla instant pudding
1 12-ounce Cool Whip®
walnuts, chopped

Make cake according to directions and bake in 9 x 13 pan. Cool to lukewarm, poke holes in top with a fork. Mix pineapple and juice with brown sugar, boil for 5 minutes. Spoon over cake. Make pudding according to package directions, minus 1/2 cup milk. Spread this on pineapple layer, spread Cool Whip® over pudding and sprinkle with walnuts. Refrigerate overnight or several hours. Very moist and delicious.

Rhubarb Cake

1-3/4 cups flour
4 tablespoons sugar
3/4 cup margarine

Mix and bake in a 9 x 13 pan at 325° for 25 minutes. Cool.

4 egg yolks
1-1/2 cups sugar
2/3 cup half and half
4 tablespoons flour
4 cups rhubarb, sliced

Beat together yolks and sugar, add the rest of the ingredients and cook, stirring constantly until thick. Cool and pour over crust.

4 egg whites
1/2 teaspoon cream of tartar
8 tablespoons sugar
1/2 teaspoon vanilla

Beat whites and cream of tartar until soft peaks form, then beat in sugar and vanilla until stiff. Pour over yolk mixture. Bake at 350° for 20 minutes.

Fruit Cocktail Cake

1-1/2 cups flour
1 cup sugar
1 teaspoon baking powder
1 teaspoon baking soda
1/2 teaspoon salt
1 egg
2 cups fruit cocktail (with juice)
1 cup brown sugar
1 cup walnuts, chopped

Mix dry ingredients well, beat in egg and fruit cocktail. Mix well. Pour into greased 9 x 13 pan. Cover with brown sugar and walnuts. Bake at 350° for 45 minutes. Serve warm or cold.

Fuzzy Navel Cake

1 can peaches, chopped and drained, reserve liquid
1/2 cup peach schnapps
1/4 cup orange juice
1 cup sugar

Combine above in covered glass container for 24 hours.

1 package yellow cake mix
1 small package instant French vanilla pudding
4 eggs
2/3 cup oil
1 cup chopped peaches, from above mixture
1/3 cup liquid from above mixture
1 cup pecans, chopped

Mix ingredients and place in greased and floured bundt pan. Bake at 350° for 40 minutes. Glaze: Combine 1/4 cup remaining liquid mixture and 1-1/2 cups powdered sugar.

Ila's Rhubarb Cake

1-1/2 cups sugar
1 egg
1/2 cup shortening
1 cup buttermilk
1 teaspoon vanilla
1/2 teaspoon salt
1 teaspoon baking soda
2 cups flour
2 cups raw rhubarb, diced
cinnamon
sugar

Cream sugar, egg and shortening. Add milk and vanilla, beat well. Add remaining ingredients, except for the rhubarb. When completely mixed fold in rhubarb. Put into greased 9 x 13 pan, sprinkle with cinnamon and sugar. Bake at 350° for 45 minutes.

Apple Cake

2 tablespoons butter
1/2 cup sugar
1 egg
3/4 cup milk
1 teaspoon baking powder
2 cups flour
apples, peeled and sliced
2 tablespoons flour
1 cup sugar
cream or half and half

Mix the butter, 1/2 cup sugar, egg, milk, baking powder and flour well, put in greased 9 x 13 pan. Cover with enough apples to fill pan. Mix flour and 1 cup sugar and sprinkle on apples. Pour cream or half and half over all, drizzle as you would a glaze. Bake at 325° for 1 hour.

Cotton Pickin' Cake

1 package yellow cake mix
1 can mandarin oranges with juice
1/2 cup oil
4 eggs

Mix, and put into 2 greased 10 inch pans. Bake at 350° for about 25-30 minutes. Cool and cut each layer in half. You now have 4. Frost with following frosting recipe.

1 French vanilla instant pudding (3-ounce)
1 can crushed pineapple, with juice
9 ounces Cool Whip®
1/2 cup walnuts, chopped

Mix pudding and pineapple with juice and set until thick. Add Cool Whip® and walnuts.

Pineapple Cake

1-1/2 cups sugar
2 cups flour
1 teaspoon baking soda
1 teaspoon salt
1 20-ounce can crushed pineapple, undrained
1 cup brown sugar
1/2 cup nuts, chopped

Mix together first five ingredients and pour into 7 x 11 greased pan. Combine brown sugar and nuts and place on top of cake. Bake at 350° for 30 minutes.

Topping:
1-1/2 sticks margarine
1/2 cup sugar
1 small can evaporated milk
1 teaspoon vanilla

Combine and heat until it comes to a boil. Simmer until it thickens. Pour over pineapple cake while it is still hot.

Poor Man's Cake

1 cup sugar
1/2 cup shortening
1/2 teaspoon cloves or allspice
3/4 teaspoon nutmeg
1 teaspoon cinnamon
1 cup cold water
1 cup raisins
2 cups flour
1 teaspoon baking soda
a pinch of salt
1/2 cup floured walnuts

Boil the sugar, shortening, cloves or allspice, nutmeg, cinnamon, water and raisins for 5 minutes. Cool and add flour, baking soda and salt. Beat well and add walnuts. Bake in a loaf pan at 375° for 45 minutes or until done.

Carrot Cake

This is Aunt Didde's recipe and it's delicious!

4 eggs, well beaten
1-1/2 cups oil
3 cups carrots, grated
2 cups sugar
2 cups flour
2 teaspoons baking soda
2 teaspoons cinnamon
1 cup coconut
1/2 cup nuts, chopped

Combine eggs, oil, carrots and sugar. Sift together the flour, baking soda and cinnamon, add carrot mixture. Stir in coconut and nuts. Bake at 350° for 55 minutes.

Frosting:
1 8-ounce package cream cheese
1 stick margarine
1 pound powdered sugar
1 teaspoon vanilla

Mix together the cream cheese and margarine, add powdered sugar and vanilla. If it needs to be thinner, add milk, just a little at a time.

Apricot Nectar Cake

The recipe came from a dear lady from Eufala, Alabama.

1 lemon cake mix
4 eggs
1/2 cup sugar
1/2 cup oil
1 cup apricot nectar
3 tablespoons lemon juice
1 cup powdered sugar

Mix everything together except lemon juice and powdered sugar. Pour into greased tube or bundt pan. Bake at 325° for 1 hour. While still hot, glaze with mixture of the lemon juice and powdered sugar. This is a wonderful moist cake.

Apple Walnut Pudding Cake

This recipe came from dear Marie LaFave. Just can't say enough about that lady.

1 cup sugar
1/4 pound margarine, softened
1 egg, unbeaten
2 large unpeeled apples
1 cup flour
1 teaspoon baking soda
1 teaspoon cinnamon
1/4 teaspoon salt
1/2 cup walnuts, chopped

Beat sugar, margarine and egg. Shred or chop apples, medium coarse. Add apples, dry ingredients and walnuts. Pour into 9 inch square pan. Bake at 350° for 45 minutes or until done. Serve warm with cream sauce.

Cream Sauce:
1 cup sugar
1/2 cup margarine
1/2 cup half and half or light cream
1-1/2 teaspoons vanilla
dash of nutmeg

Combine sugar, margarine and half and half or light cream. Cook slowly until thick. Add vanilla and nutmeg. Makes 1-1/2 cups.

Rainbow Cake (Jello® Cake)

1 white cake mix
1 small package Jello®, any flavor
1 cup boiling water
1 cup cold water

Prepare cake according to package directions. Bake in greased 9 x 13 inch pan for 30-35 minutes at 350°. Cool 15 minutes. Then poke with a fork at 1/2 inch intervals. Dissolve Jello® in boiling water and add cold water. Mix well and pour over cake in pan. Chill 3-4 hours and top with Cool Whip®.

Plum Pudding

1 cup brown sugar
2 eggs
1 cup suet
1 cup buttermilk
2 cups flour
1 cup raisins, ground or chopped
3/4 teaspoon salt
1 teaspoon baking soda
1/2 teaspoon cloves
1/2 teaspoon nutmeg
1 teaspoon cinnamon

Mix all ingredients together, pour into greased pans or cans and bake at 350° until done, about 50-60 minutes. Serve warm with the cinnamon sauce found below.

Cinnamon Sauce:
3/4 cup sugar
1-1/2 cups apple juice or water
cornstarch to thicken
1 teaspoon cinnamon
1 teaspoon vanilla
1 tablespoon margarine

Bring sugar and juice or water to a boil, thicken with cornstarch and add rest of ingredients. *If you use apple juice instead of water this is a great sauce over ice cream. Perhaps served in a crispy flour tortilla bowl dusted with cinnamon and sugar.

*I'm at the age where I have nothing to do with natural foods.
I need all the preservatives I can get!!!*

Date Nut Torte

I remember loving this as a child, so I searched to find the lost recipe.

1 cup dates, chopped
1 cup nuts, chopped
2 eggs, lightly beaten
2 rounded tablespoons flour
3/4 cup corn syrup

Mix together and bake at 350° until toothpick inserted in the center comes out clean. About 35-45 minutes. Serve with the following topping.

Topping:
1 cup sugar
1 egg, well beaten
1 tablespoon vinegar
1/2 cup butter
1/2 cup water
1 teaspoon vanilla

Combine and cook slowly till slightly thickened.

Oatmeal Spice Cake

This is a wonderful old recipe that was used often in my Grandmother's day.

1/2 cup butter
1 cup brown sugar
2 eggs, beaten
1-1/2 teaspoons baking soda
1 teaspoon cinnamon
1/2 teaspoon salt
1/2 teaspoon nutmeg
2 tablespoons dark molasses
1 cup water
1 cup oatmeal
1-1/2 cups flour

Cream together the butter, sugar and eggs. Add baking soda, cinnamon, salt, nutmeg and molasses and mix. Add the water, oatmeal and flour. Pour into a 9 x 13 pan and bake at 350° for 35 minutes. Top with one of the two cooked coconut, walnut icings found at the end of this chapter.

Bacardi® Rum Cake

> 1 cup pecans or walnuts, chopped
> 1 yellow cake mix
> 1 small package instant French vanilla pudding
> 4 eggs
> 1/2 cup cold water
> 1/2 cup oil
> 1/2 cup Bacardi® dark rum

Preheat oven to 325°. Grease and flour 10 inch tube or 12 cup bundt pan. Sprinkle nuts over bottom of pan. Mix all ingredients and pour batter over nuts. Bake 1 hour. Set on rack to cool. Invert onto serving plate. Prick top and drizzle or brush evenly with glaze on top and sides.

> Glaze:
> 1/2 pound butter
> 1/2 cup water
> 1 cup sugar
> 1/2 cup Bacardi® dark rum

Melt butter and stir in water and sugar. Boil 5 minutes, stirring constantly. Stir in rum. Garnish cake with whipped cream.

Nellie's Pound Cake

Nellie Smith is my nephew Freddie's grandma. She's straight from the South which is why she's such a good cook.

> 2 sticks butter
> 3 cups sugar
> 4 eggs
> 1 cup sour cream + 2 tablespoons lemon juice
> 1/4 teaspoon salt
> 1/4 teaspoon baking soda

Cream butter and sugar together until smooth. Add eggs, one at a time. Add all other ingredients. Bake in an angel food cake pan for 1-1/2 hours at 300°. Cool, remove from the pan, and enjoy. Thank you, Nellie.

Sunshine Cake

6 eggs, separated
pinch of salt
1 cup sugar
4 tablespoons water
1 cup flour
1 rounded teaspoon baking powder

Beat yolks, salt and sugar for 10 minutes. Add 2 tablespoons water and beat hard. Add 2 more tablespoons water and beat again. Add flour. Beat egg whites until foamy and then add baking powder. Beat until it stands in peaks. Slowly fold into egg yolk mixture. Bake in an angel food pan at 250° for 1/2 hour, then at 300° for 1/2 hour. Cool well before removing from pan.

Never let a difficulty stop you. It may only be
sand on the path to stop you from slipping.

Chocolate Waldorf Cake

This is a scrumptious cake that I made for Julie every year on her birthday.

1 angel food cake mix
3 half pints of whipping cream
1-1/2 cups powdered sugar
3/4 cup cocoa
1/4 teaspoon salt
chopped nuts

Bake angel food cake according to directions. Cool and slice off the top about 1 to 1-1/2 inches down. Scoop out to make a trench in the cake. In chilled bowl, whip the whipping cream, powdered sugar, cocoa and salt until stiff. Divide filling in half and fold in chopped nuts into one half. Fill trench with this half. Place top back on cake and frost the top and sides with the rest of the filling. The leftover cake pieces makes a great cook's treat.

Chocolate Butter Cream Frosting

1/2 - 3/4 cup cocoa
6 tablespoons butter
2-2/3 cups powdered sugar
1/3 cup milk
1 teaspoon vanilla
nuts, chopped, optional

Mix together and frost.

Flour Frosting

2-1/2 tablespoons flour
1/2 cup milk
1/2 cup margarine
3/4 cup sugar
1 teaspoon vanilla

Whisk flour and milk in saucepan until smooth. Cook until thick, stirring constantly. Cool. Beat together the margarine and sugar. Add cooled flour mixture. Beat until light and add vanilla.

Butter Cream Frosting

This is the frosting I use for decorating cakes.

1 cup Crisco®
1 cup butter
pinch of salt
about 1 teaspoon vanilla
1-2 pound bag powdered sugar
about 1/3 cup water

Mix the Crisco® and butter well until the color is a cream color. Add salt and vanilla. Add powdered sugar and water. Mix slowly until all the sugar is mixed in, then beat on high till the frosting is very nearly white. This frosting is never snow white, but I think the taste is superior. Also, I find that if I use butter instead of margarine, it will get whiter.

Our Light And Creamy Icing

1 cup milk
4 teaspoons cornstarch

Cook together until thick. Remove from heat and cool.

Cream together:
1 cup sugar
1 stick butter
1/2 cup shortening
2 teaspoons vanilla

Combine cooked and creamed ingredients and whip for at least 5 minutes or until the frosting is very creamy. In the beginning it may look as thought it has separated, but just keep beating. Garnish with the following Ganache recipe.

Ganache

1 cup chocolate chips
2 tablespoons butter
1/4 cup milk

Melt chocolate chips with butter and milk. Stir until smooth. Cool. This works best on a layer cake. Frost cake with the Light and Creamy Icing recipe above and drizzle this chocolate ganache around the edges and down the sides. I like to sprinkle nuts on top.

Penuche Icing

1/2 cup butter
1 cup packed brown sugar
1/4 cup milk
1-3/4 to 2 cups powdered sugar

Melt butter, add brown sugar. Boil over low heat for 2 minutes stirring constantly. Stir in milk and stir until it comes to a boil. Cool to lukewarm. Gradually add powdered sugar. Beat until spreading consistency. If it gets too thick, add a little hot water.

Chocolate Butter Cream Frosting

6 tablespoons margarine, softened
3/4 cup cocoa
2- 2/3 cups powdered sugar
1/3 cup milk
1 teaspoon vanilla

Cream margarine and add cocoa and sugar alternately with milk. Beat to spreading consistency. Add more milk if needed. Blend in vanilla. Makes about 2 cups.

Creamy Chocolate Frosting

1 8-ounce package cream cheese
1 teaspoon vanilla
pinch of salt
5 cups powdered sugar
1/2 cup cocoa
1 tablespoons milk

Combine cream cheese, vanilla and salt. Mix well until blended. Add sugar and cocoa alternately with milk, beating until light and fluffy.

Chocolate Sheet Cake Icing

1 stick margarine
4 tablespoons cocoa
3 tablespoons buttermilk
3 tablespoons milk
1 pound powdered sugar
1 teaspoon vanilla
1 cup nuts, chopped

Beat until very creamy. Sprinkle nuts on top. This is very good.

Broiled Icing

1 stick butter or margarine, melted
1 cup coconut
1/4 cup milk
1 cup brown sugar
1 teaspoon vanilla
1/2 cup nuts, chopped

Mix ingredients well until sugar is dissolved and everything is blended well. Frost the cake and place under the broiler until it bubbles. Don't let it get brown.

Cooked Coconut Pecan Frosting

This icing and the one above are both great frostings for the oatmeal cake found in this chapter.

1 can evaporated milk (not sweetened condensed)
1 cup sugar
1 egg
1 stick margarine
1 teaspoon vanilla
1 cup nuts, chopped
1-1/3 cups coconut

Mix together in a saucepan. Cook (boil slowly), for 12 minutes. Cool slightly and frost cake.

7 Minute Maple Frosting

3/4 cup maple syrup
1/4 cup sugar
1 egg white
1 teaspoon light corn syrup
1/8 teaspoon salt

Place all ingredients in top of double boiler. Beat for 1 minute with hand mixer. Place over boiling water and cook, beating constantly until it is stiff enough to stand in peaks, about 7 minutes. Keep water boiling during beating time and scrape down sides of pan often. Remove from heat and continue to beat until it is cool and of spreading consistency.

Chocolate Filling For Cake

This is a very good filling to use in place of frosting between cake layers.

1 cup milk
1-1/2 squares bitter chocolate
3/4 cup sugar
2 tablespoons flour
1/2 teaspoon salt
1 egg yolk
6 tablespoons butter
1/2 teaspoon vanilla

Heat milk and chocolate in double boiler. Add and beat until blended the sugar, flour and salt. Add egg yolk, butter and vanilla. Cook, stirring constantly, until very thick. Cool and spread between cake layers. Very good.

Snow On The Mountain Frosting

This is the vanilla version of the above recipe.

1-1/4 cups light corn syrup
2 egg whites, room temperature
1/8 teaspoon salt
1 teaspoon vanilla

Bring syrup to a boil and remove from heat. Beat egg whites until foamy. Add salt and continue beating until soft peaks form. Slowly pour syrup into egg white mixture beating constantly on high. Beat until soft peaks form and add vanilla while still beating. Spread on cake.

Lemon Filling For Cake (Lemon Curd)

2-1/2 tablespoons lemon juice
6 tablespoons orange juice
1/3 cup water
1/2 cup sugar
2 tablespoons flour
1/8 teaspoon salt
3 egg yolks
1/2 teaspoon lemon zest

Combine and cook in a double boiler until very thick. Stir constantly. Cool and spread between cake layers.

Cookies
& Bars

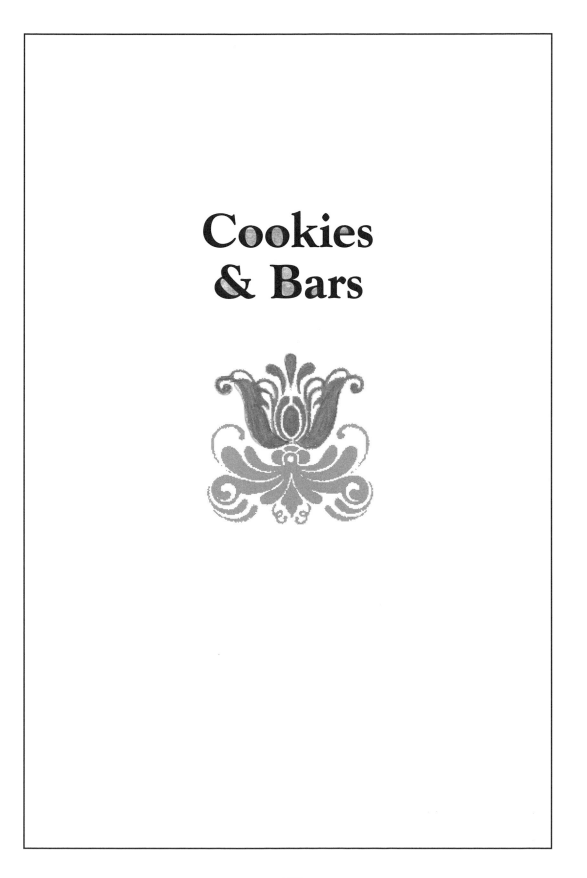

Toll House® Cookies

3/4 cup sugar
3/4 cup brown sugar
1 cup margarine
2 eggs
1 teaspoon vanilla
1-1/2 to 1-3/4 cups flour
1/2 teaspoon baking powder
1 teaspoon baking soda
1 teaspoon salt
1 teaspoon water
2 cups quick oatmeal
12 ounces chocolate chips

Cream sugars and margarine. Add eggs and rest of ingredients, except oatmeal and chips. Mix well and then add oatmeal. Mix and add chips. Drop on ungreased sheet pan and bake at 350° for 10-12 minutes.

Dish Pan Cookies

2 cups brown sugar
2 cups sugar
2 cups oil
4 eggs
2 teaspoons vanilla
4 cups flour
2 teaspoons baking soda
1 teaspoon salt
4 cups corn flakes
1-1/2 cups oatmeal

Mix together sugars, oil, eggs and vanilla. Sift together dry ingredients, except corn flakes and oatmeal and add to sugar mixture. Stir in corn flakes (crush then measure) and oats last. Make into balls and press flat. Bake at 350° for 8-10 minutes. Makes 10 dozen.

Orange Cookies

1-1/2 cups brown sugar
1 cup shortening
2 eggs, beaten
1 teaspoon vanilla
1 cup sour milk with 1 teaspoon baking soda
1 tablespoon grated orange rind
3 cups flour
2 teaspoons baking powder
1/2 teaspoon salt

Mix sugar, shortening, and eggs. Add rest of ingredients and drop on greased pan with teaspoon. Bake at 400° for 12-15 minutes. Frost with following icing recipe.

Frosting:
2 cups powdered sugar
3 tablespoons orange juice
1 teaspoon grated orange rind
3 tablespoons melted butter

Mix together and frost warm cookies.

Quick Sugar Cookies

Mix together:
1/2 cup margarine
1/2 cup shortening
1 cup sugar
1 egg
2 teaspoons vinegar
1 teaspoon vanilla
1 teaspoon salt
2-1/2 cups flour
1/2 teaspoon baking soda
lemon zest

Roll into balls. Flatten with glass dipped in sugar. Bake at 375° for 10 minutes.

Grandma Hazel's Sugar Cookies

2 cups sugar
1-1/2 cups margarine
1 egg
1 cup sour milk
1 teaspoon baking soda
1 teaspoon vanilla
1 teaspoon lemon juice
4 cups flour

Mix all ingredients together. Chill dough. Roll out on lightly floured board. Cut out cookies and place on cookie sheet. Bake at 350° for 8-10 minutes.

Chocolate Drop Cookies

1 cup brown sugar
1/2 cup butter
1 egg, beaten
1/2 cup sour milk
1-1/2 cups flour
1/4 teaspoon salt
1/4 teaspoon baking powder
1/4 teaspoon baking soda
2 squares melted chocolate
1 cup chopped nuts

Mix in order given. Drop on greased cookie sheet with teaspoon. Bake at 350° for 12-15 minutes. Frost with icing.

Icing
1 square of chocolate
1 egg
1 tablespoon cream
about 2 cups powdered sugar

Melt chocolate in saucepan, add egg, cream and powdered sugar. Bring just to a boil, whisking to a smooth consistency. Remove from heat and cool slightly and frost warm cookies.

Chocolate Peanut Butter Surprises

1-1/2 cups flour
1/2 cup cocoa
1/2 teaspoon baking soda
1/2 cup soft butter
1/2 cup sugar
1/2 cup brown sugar
1/4 cup peanut butter
1 egg
1 tablespoon milk
1 teaspoon vanilla

Combine the flour, cocoa and baking soda, set aside. In mixer bowl, mix butter, sugars and peanut butter together until creamy. Add egg, milk and vanilla. Beat well. Gradually add flour mixture. If it becomes too thick, mix in the rest with your hands or a large spoon. Form this dough into 30-32 balls. Set aside.

Filling:
3/4 cup powdered sugar
1/2 cup peanut butter
2 tablespoons granulated sugar

Combine powdered sugar and peanut butter well. Shape it in as many chocolate balls as was made above. Slightly flatten the chocolate balls, wrap each one around a peanut butter ball, covering it completely. Put on a cookie sheet. Use a glass to dip in the sugar and flatten the cookies a bit. Bake at 350° for about 8 minutes. Cool on a rack.

Spritz

1 cup butter, softened
2/3 cup sugar
2 egg yolks
1 teaspoon almond or vanilla flavoring
1 tablespoon cream
2-1/2 cups flour

Mix everything except flour. Then gently add flour. Work in completely and put through a cookie press. Bake on a cookie sheet at 400° for 7-10 minutes.

Gingersnaps

1-1/2 cups shortening
1-1/2 cups sugar
1/2 cup brown sugar
1/2 cup light molasses
2 eggs
4 cups flour
1/2 teaspoon salt
4 teaspoons baking soda
2 teaspoons cinnamon
2 teaspoons ground cloves
2 teaspoons ginger

Cream shortening and sugars. Add molasses and eggs. Add dry ingredients and mix well. Roll into balls the size of a walnut, dip in sugar and flatten on greased cookie sheet about 2 inches apart. Bake at 375° for 14-15 minutes. Do not over bake. Makes 6-1/2 dozen.

Sour Cream Spice Cookies

This soft cookie recipe came from dear Natalie Middaugh.

1/2 cup shortening
1 cup brown sugar
1 cup white sugar
2 eggs
1 teaspoon vanilla
3 cups flour
1 teaspoon baking soda
1 teaspoon cinnamon
1/2 teaspoon ground cloves
1/2 teaspoon nutmeg
1/2 teaspoon salt
2/3 cup sour cream

Cream shortening and sugars. Add eggs and vanilla. Mix well. Sift dry ingredients together and add alternately with sour cream. Mix well. Drop by teaspoon onto a greased cookie sheet. Bake at 350° for 12-15 minutes.

Angel Cookies

1 cup shortening
1/2 cup brown sugar
1/2 cup sugar
1 egg, beaten
1 teaspoon vanilla
2 cups flour
1 teaspoon baking soda
1 teaspoon cream of tartar
1/2 teaspoon salt
1/2 cup walnuts, chopped, optional
Granulated sugar for dipping

Cream shortening and sugars. Add other ingredients in order given. Roll into balls the size of a walnut. Dip in cold water and then into sugar. Bake at 350° for 8 minutes.

One Hundred Good Cookies

1 cup sugar
1 cup brown sugar
1 cup oil
1 cup margarine
1 teaspoon salt
1 egg
1 teaspoon baking soda
1 teaspoon cream of tartar
3-1/2 cups flour
1 cup oatmeal
1 cup Rice Krispies®
1 cup chocolate chips
1 cup chopped walnuts

Beat sugars, oil, margarine, salt and egg. Add baking soda, cream of tartar and flour. Mix in rest of ingredients. Drop by teaspoonful on greased sheets. Bake at 325° for 15 minutes.

Peanut Butter Cookies

1/2 cup margarine
1/2 cup peanut butter
1/2 cup sugar
1/2 cup packed brown sugar
1 egg
1-1/4 cups flour
1/2 teaspoon baking powder
3/4 teaspoon baking soda
1/4 teaspoon salt

Mix margarine, peanut butter and sugars. Add egg and mix thoroughly. Add all dry ingredients. Chill dough. Roll dough into 1 inch balls and place on cookie sheet. Flatten and bake 350° for 10-12 minutes. Makes 3 dozen.

God made time... Man made haste.

Katie's Peanut Butter Cookies

1/2 cup butter
1 egg, slightly beaten
1 teaspoon vanilla
1/2 cup creamy peanut butter
3/4 cup salted peanuts, chopped
3/4 cup brown sugar
3/4 cup sugar
1-1/2 cups flour
1 teaspoon baking powder
1 teaspoon salt
3/4 cup peanut butter chips

Cream butter, egg and vanilla. Add peanut butter. Add peanuts, sugars, flour, baking powder, salt and chips. Stir until well blended. Drop by rounded teaspoon onto a greased cookie sheet. Bake at 350° for 11-13 minutes.

Peanut Butter Fudge Tarts

This little bit of heaven was sort of a late comer, but I just had to make sure it was part of this book.

prepared peanut butter or sugar cookie dough
  (homemade, bag mix or from a refrigerated roll)
1/2 cup chocolate chips
1/4 cup sweetened condensed milk

Drop peanut butter cookie or sugar cookie dough by the 1/2 teaspoon into a mini muffin pan. Bake at 350° for 9 minutes. Remove from the oven and make a little well in the center with the back of a teaspoon or a melon-baller. Melt the chocolate chips and milk together and fill the little peanut butter cups. Return to the oven for 2 more minutes. Take out of the oven and cool slightly before removing from the tins.

Hershey® Kiss Cookies

1/2 cup sugar
1/2 cup brown sugar
1/2 cup margarine
1/2 cup peanut butter
1 egg
2 tablespoons milk
1 teaspoon vanilla
1-3/4 cups flour
1 teaspoon baking soda
1/2 teaspoon salt
Hershey® kisses, unwrapped

Mix all ingredients, except Hershey® kisses and roll into balls. Roll in sugar and place on cookie sheet. Bake at 350° for 12 minutes. As soon as they come out of the oven, push a Hershey® kiss in the center of each, let cool.

Refrigerator Cookies

1 cup butter
2/3 cup brown sugar
1 egg
1 teaspoon vanilla
1 teaspoon salt
2-1/2 cups flour
sugar

Mix together the butter, brown sugar, egg, vanilla and salt. Add flour a little at a time. Knead a little and roll into a log. Cut into 3 logs. Wrap in plastic wrap and chill overnight. Roll each log in sugar and slice. Bake at 350° for 15-20 minutes. Sometimes I slice them and lay in sugar before baking.

Crunchy Praline Cookies

2 cups flour
1/4 teaspoon baking soda
1/4 teaspoon salt
1/2 cup butter
1 cup brown sugar
1 egg
1 tablespoon orange juice

Topping:
1-1/2 cups chopped pecans
1/2 cup dark brown sugar
1/2 teaspoon cinnamon
1/4 cup sour cream

Mix the flour, baking soda and salt together, set aside. Cream together the butter and sugar. Add the egg, orange juice and flour mixture, set aside. To make topping, mix together the pecans, brown sugar, cinnamon and sour cream. Roll cookies into small balls, about 1/2 inch. Make a well in center of each and fill with about 1/4 teaspoon topping mixture. Bake at 350° for 8-10 minutes.

Pecan Tart Cookies

Rosanne Weber brought these for a cookie exchange one year and they're wonderful.

1 cup butter
1 8-ounce package cream cheese
2 cups flour
1/2 teaspoon baking powder
1 cup brown sugar
1/2 cup sugar
1 teaspoon salt
2 eggs, beaten
2 tablespoons milk
1 teaspoon vanilla
1/2 cup margarine, melted
1 cup pecans, chopped

Mix butter and cream cheese. Add flour and baking powder. Mix well and chill dough for 3 hours. To make filling, mix the sugars, salt, eggs, milk, vanilla and margarine. Stir all well and add pecans.

Use a small muffin tin, well greased. Roll out dough on floured surface fairly thin and cut with glass top. Press dough lightly into muffin tin. Fill each tart with 1 teaspoon of the filling and bake at 350° for 10-15 minutes or until light brown. Makes 5 dozen.

Heath Bars

saltine crackers
2 sticks margarine
1 cup brown sugar
1 teaspoon vanilla
chocolate chips or chocolate bars
nuts, chopped, optional

Line cookie sheet with saltine crackers. Bring the margarine, brown sugar and vanilla to a boil and boil for 4 minutes. Pour over saltine crackers. Bake at 350° for 4 minutes. Remove from oven and top with chocolate chips or chocolate bars. Let melt for a few minutes and then spread over the top. You can sprinkle nut meats over the top of the chocolate. Immediately put crackers on waxed paper to cool. They keep well in the freezer.

Rice Krispie® Cookies

1 cup margarine
1 cup sugar
1-1/2 cups flour
1/2 teaspoon baking soda
1/2 teaspoon baking powder
1 teaspoon vanilla
1 cup Rice Krispies®

Mix all ingredients except the cereal with a mixer, then stir in the Rice Krispies® with a spoon. Roll into balls. Dip a glass into flour and flatten to about 1/4 inch. They will spread to about 1/8 inch thick. Bake at 325° for 12-15 minutes. This is a very good crisp cookie.

Chocolate Bittersweets

1/2 cup margarine
1/2 cup powdered sugar
1/4 teaspoon salt
1 teaspoon vanilla
1-1/4 cups flour
4 ounces cream cheese
2 tablespoons flour
1 teaspoon vanilla
1/2 cup walnuts, chopped
1 cup powdered sugar

Mix together margarine, powdered sugar, salt, vanilla and flour and make into small balls. Flatten with thumb to the size of a quarter, leaving a slight indentation in center. Bake at 350° for 12-15 minutes. Mix cream cheese, flour, vanilla, walnuts and powdered sugar together to make filling and place in the center of the cookies while warm.

Frosting:
1/2 cup chocolate chips
2 tablespoons margarine
2 tablespoons water
1/2 cup powdered sugar

Melt chips, margarine and add water and sugar. Spread on filling.

Easter Basket Cookies

1 cup sugar
1 cup Karo® syrup
1-1/2 cups peanut butter
1 cup chocolate chips
4 cups Rice Krispies®
green colored coconut
colored mini jelly beans

Bring the sugar and Karo® syrup to a boil, add the peanut butter and chocolate chips. Stir until melted, then add 4 cups Rice Krispies®. Shape into little nests or baskets. Decorate with the colored coconut and jelly beans. This is a great project for little fingers at Easter time.

Children never exaggerate... They just remember BIG.

Pinwheels

3/4 cup margarine
3/4 cup sugar
1 egg yolk
1/2 teaspoon vanilla
1-3/4 cups flour
1-1/2 teaspoons baking powder
1/2 teaspoon salt
1 tablespoon milk
1 square chocolate, melted

Cream margarine and sugar. Add yolk and vanilla, and blend. Add dry ingredients and milk. Divide dough, put chocolate in half. Refrigerate until firm and easy to handle. Roll both 1/8 inch thick on well powdered sugared surface. Place one on top of the other and roll as for a jelly roll. Wrap in wax paper. Refrigerate overnight or several hours. Slice into 1/8 inch slices. Place on greased sheet pans and bake at 375° for 8 minutes. Makes about 8 dozen.

Birds Nests

1 cup margarine
1/2 cup brown sugar
2 egg yolks (save whites)
1 teaspoon vanilla
2 cups flour
walnuts, finely chopped
Jelly or jam

Mix everything well except nuts and jelly. Chill. Roll into balls and dip in slightly beaten egg whites, then in the walnuts. Place on baking sheet and press thumb in the center. Fill with jelly. Bake at 350° for 10 minutes, until set. I sometimes put in the jelly after the first 5 minutes.

Caramel Apple Bars

Base:
2 cups flour
2 cups quick oatmeal
1-1/2 cups packed brown sugar
1 teaspoon baking soda
1-1/4 cups butter, melted

Filling:
1-1/2 cups caramel ice cream topping
1/2 cup flour
2 cups apples, peeled and chopped
1/2 cup nuts, chopped

Combine all base ingredients and press half into a 15 x 10 inch pan (half sheet). Bake at 350° for 8 minutes.

Combine caramel and flour. Bring to a boil stirring constantly, boil 3-5 minutes until it thickens slightly. Sprinkle apples and nuts over baked base and pour caramel mixture over the top. Sprinkle remaining base mixture on top and bake at 350° for 20-25 minutes. Cool 30 minutes. Refrigerate 30 minutes or until set.

Banana Bars

1/2 cup butter, softened
2 cups sugar
3 eggs
1-1/2 cups mashed bananas (about 3)
1 teaspoon vanilla
2 cups flour
1 teaspoon baking soda
pinch of salt

Cream butter and sugar, add eggs, bananas and vanilla. Combine with flour, baking soda and salt. Pour into a greased 10 x 15 jelly roll pan. Bake at 350° for 25 minutes or until bars test done. Cool.

Frosting:
1/2 cup butter
1 8-ounce package cream cheese
4 cups powdered sugar
2 teaspoons vanilla

Cream butter and cream cheese. Add sugar and vanilla. Beat well and spread on bars.

Butterscotch Cheesecake Bars

1 12-ounce bag butterscotch chips
1/3 cup margarine
2 cups graham cracker crumbs
1/2 cup walnuts, chopped
1 8-ounce package cream cheese
1 can sweetened condensed milk
1 teaspoon vanilla
1 egg

Melt chips and margarine. Stir in crumbs and nuts. Press 1/2 mixture in a 9 x 13 greased pan. Beat cheese until fluffy and add milk, vanilla and egg. Mix well and pour into pan and top with rest of crumbs. Bake at 350° for 25-30 minutes. Refrigerate.

Carrot Bars

These are Molly's bars and they really are wonderful.

4 eggs
2 teaspoons baking soda
1 teaspoon salt
2-1/2 cups flour
2 cups sugar
2 teaspoons cinnamon
1-1/2 cups oil
3 small jars baby food carrots
walnuts, chopped

Mix together and pour into greased jelly roll pan. Bake at 350° for 25 minutes. Frost with the following frosting recipe.

Frosting:
3-1/2 cups powdered sugar
1 8-ounce package cream cheese
1 teaspoon vanilla
1 stick margarine, melted

Mix and spread over bars.

Pecan Pie Bars

2 cups flour
1/2 cup powdered sugar
1 cup cold margarine
1 can sweetened condensed milk
1 egg
1 teaspoon vanilla
1 6-ounce package butter brickle chips
1 cup pecans, chopped

Combine flour and sugar. Cut in margarine until crumbly. Press on bottom of 9 x 13 pan and bake at 350° for 15 minutes. Beat milk, egg and vanilla. Stir in chips and pecans. Spread over crust and bake 25 minutes or until golden brown. Chill and store in refrigerator.

Pecan Fingers

1 cup margarine
1/2 cup powdered sugar
2 cups flour
1 cup pecans, chopped
2 teaspoons vanilla

Mix well. Roll into finger shapes or balls. Bake at 350° for 15 minutes. Roll in powdered sugar.

Pumpkin Pie Bars

These are THE BEST! I got the recipe from Helen Peterson.

Mix until crumbly:
1 cup flour
1/2 cup oatmeal
1/2 cup brown sugar
1/2 cup butter

Press into 9 x 13 pan and bake at 350° for 15 minutes.

Filling:
1 pound can pumpkin
1 13-1/2 ounce can evaporated milk
2 eggs
3/4 cup sugar
1/2 teaspoon salt
1 teaspoon cinnamon
1/2 teaspoon ginger
1/4 teaspoon ground cloves

Mix filling ingredients and pour over crust. Bake this for 20 minutes.

Combine:
1/2 cup walnuts, chopped
1/2 cup brown sugar
2 tablespoons butter

Sprinkle over bars and bake 15-20 minutes more until filling is set.

Apple Pizza

3 cups flour
1/2 teaspoon salt
1/2 teaspoon baking powder
3/4 cup margarine
3 egg yolks, saving whites
1/2 cup water
10-12 apples, peeled and sliced
sugar
cinnamon
lemon juice to taste
egg whites, beaten

Combine the flour, salt, baking powder, margarine, yolks and water, mix well and roll half to fit jelly roll pan. Toss together the apples, sugar, cinnamon and lemon, and arrange on bottom crust. Roll out other half of dough. Place over apples. Brush with beaten egg whites. Bake at 350° until golden brown, 20-30 minutes. Top with a glaze of powdered sugar and milk.

Lemon Bars

2 cups flour
1/2 cup powdered sugar
1 cup margarine
1/3 cup lemon juice
2 cups sugar
4 eggs, beaten
1/4 cup flour
1 teaspoon baking powder

Cream 2 cups flour, powdered sugar and margarine. Pat into greased 9 x 13 pan. Bake at 350° for 15-20 minutes. Mix all the rest and pour over crust. Bake at 30-35 minutes. Sprinkle with powdered sugar.

Seven Layer Bars
(Also called Magic Cookie Bars)

1 stick margarine
1-1/4 cups graham cracker crumbs
1 cup butterscotch chips
1 cup coconut
1 cup chocolate chips
1 can sweetened condensed milk
1 cup nuts, chopped

In a 9 x 13 pan, melt margarine. Add graham cracker crumbs. Mix and spread on bottom of pan. Top with butterscotch chips, then a layer of coconut and a layer of chocolate chips (I prefer the mini chips). Cover with the sweetened condensed milk and sprinkle on nuts. Bake at 350° for 25 minutes. **Do not over bake.**

Chocolate Chip Bars

1 8-ounce package cream cheese, softened
1/2 cup margarine
1/2 cup brown sugar
1/4 cup sugar
1 egg
1 teaspoon vanilla
1 cup oatmeal
2/3 cup flour
1/2 teaspoon baking powder
pinch of salt
6 ounces chocolate chips
1/4 cup walnuts, chopped

Combine cream cheese, margarine and sugars. Add egg and vanilla. Add dry ingredients and mix well. Stir in chips and nuts. Put in 9 x 13 pan and bake at 350° for 30 minutes.

Date Bars

1-3/4 cups oatmeal
1-1/2 cups flour
1 cup brown sugar
1 teaspoon baking soda
1/2 teaspoon salt
3/4 cup butter
3/4 cup dates or raisins
1 cup sugar
1 cup water
3/4 cup walnuts, chopped

Mix oatmeal, flour, 1 cup sugar, baking soda and salt, work in butter thoroughly. Pack half into an 8 inch pan. Cook the dates or raisins, sugar and water on medium heat, until it's thick. Cool and add the walnuts. Spread on crust. Sprinkle the remaining crust on top of the dates and press down firmly. Bake at 375° for 40 minutes.

Chocolate Delight Bars

1/2 cup margarine
1 egg yolk
1 tablespoon water
1-1/4 cups flour
1 teaspoon sugar
2 teaspoons baking powder
1 cup chocolate chips
2 eggs
3/4 cup sugar
6 tablespoons margarine, melted
2 teaspoons vanilla
2 cups walnuts, chopped

Beat 1/2 cup margarine, egg yolk and water. Stir in flour, sugar and baking powder. Press into 9 x 13 pan and bake 10 minutes at 350°. Sprinkle chocolate chips over the top. Beat 2 eggs, sugar, margarine, vanilla and walnuts. Spread on top and bake at 350° for 30 minutes.

Chocolate Almond Coconut Bars

1 cup flour
1/2 cup brown sugar
1/4 cup margarine, softened
1 cup flaked coconut
1 can sweetened condensed milk (divided in half)
2 cups whole blanched almonds

Combine flour, sugar and margarine and mix until crumbly. Press into greased 9 x 13 pan. Mix coconut and 1/2 can of milk and pour over the crust. Lay almonds evenly over coconut. Bake at 350° for 20-25 minutes until golden. Cool 10 minutes.

Frosting:
1 cup chocolate chips
remaining sweetened condensed milk
1/2 teaspoon vanilla

Melt chocolate chips and the rest of the milk. Stir in vanilla. Spread over warm bars. Chill until firm.

Chocolate Peanut Butter Squares

1 cup peanut butter, chunky or creamy
1 cup chocolate chips
1/2 cup margarine, cut into small pieces
1 bag mini marshmallows
2 cups Rice Krispies® cereal

Spray 8 x 8 pan with pan spray. Put peanut butter, chips and margarine in 3 quart microwave safe bowl. Microwave uncovered on high for 2-1/2 minutes until margarine melts and chips look soft and glossy, but still hold their shape. Stir until smooth, then stir in marshmallows. Microwave 45-60 seconds. Marshmallows will be slightly melted. Stir to mix, then stir in cereal until well blended. Put into prepared pan. Cool 2-3 hours until firm.

Rocky Road Bars

1 square chocolate
1/2 cup margarine
1 cup sugar
1 teaspoon vanilla
1 cup flour
1/2 to 1 cup walnuts, chopped
1 teaspoon baking powder
2 eggs

Melt chocolate and margarine. Add other ingredients and mix well. Spread into greased and floured 9 x 13 pan.

Filling:
1 8-ounce package cream cheese
1/2 cup sugar
2 tablespoons flour
1/4 cup margarine, softened
1 egg
1/2 teaspoon vanilla
1/4 cup nuts, chopped
1 cup chocolate chips
2 cups mini marshmallows

Combine cream cheese, sugar, flour, margarine, egg and vanilla until fluffy. Add nuts and spread over base. Sprinkle with chocolate chips and bake at 350° for 25-35 minutes. Sprinkle with marshmallows and bake 2 minutes longer. Frost immediately with the following:

Frosting:
1/4 cup margarine, melted
1 square chocolate, melted
2 ounces cream cheese
1/4 cup milk
1 pound powdered sugar
1 teaspoon vanilla

Mix margarine, chocolate, cheese, and milk. Add sugar and vanilla. Blend well, pour over marshmallows and swirl together. Store in refrigerator.

Hershey's® Brownies

1 cup sugar
4 eggs
1 teaspoon vanilla
1 stick margarine
1 large can Hershey's® Syrup
1 cup flour
1/2 cup nuts, chopped

Mix all together. Bake in greased 9 x 13 pan at 350° for 40-45 minutes.

Frosting:
1-1/2 cups sugar
6 tablespoons margarine
6 tablespoons milk
1 cup chocolate chips

Bring sugar, margarine and milk to a boil, then add chocolate chips. Boil for 30 seconds. Beat and spread on brownies.

Special K® Bars

6 or 7 cups Special K® cereal
1 stick margarine
1 cup sugar
1 cup Karo® syrup
1-1/2 cups peanut butter

Place the cereal in a large bowl, set aside. In a saucepan, bring the margarine, sugar and Karo® syrup to a rolling boil. Then add peanut butter. Mix well and pour over cereal. Mix all together and put into buttered 9 x 13 pan.

Topping:
6 ounces chocolate chips
6 ounces peanut butter chips or butterscotch chips

Melt the chocolate chips and peanut butter or butterscotch chips and spread over bars. This is a good way to get rid of little bits of cereal, because you can use more than one kind.

Desserts, Pies
& Candies

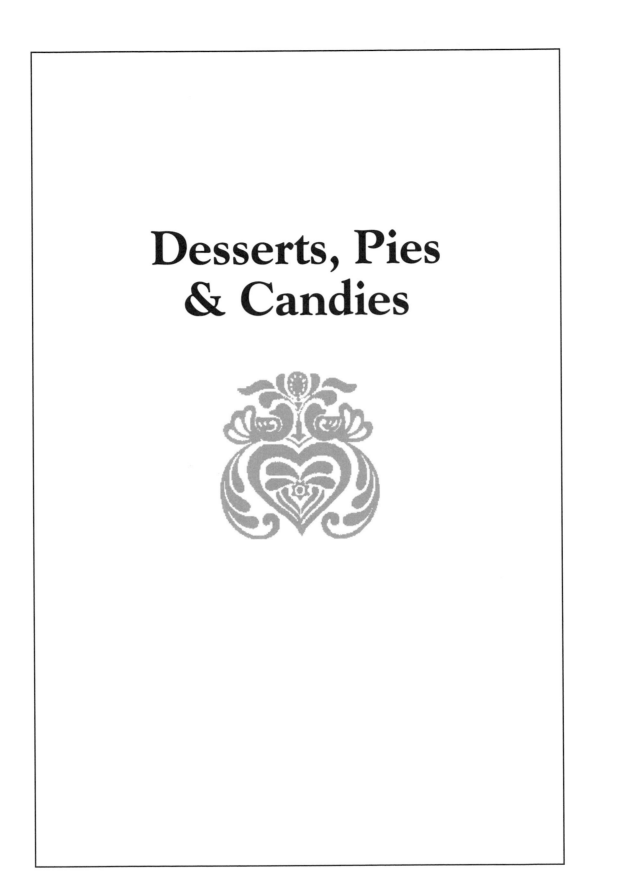

Pistachio Dessert

1 cup flour
1 stick of margarine
2 tablespoons sugar
1/4 cup walnuts, chopped

Mix together like pie crust and press into 9 x 13 pan. Bake at 350° for 15 minutes. Cool. Top with:

1 8-ounce package cream cheese
2/3 cup powdered sugar
1/2 of large container Cool Whip®

Mix cream cheese with powdered sugar, add Cool Whip®. Spread on cooled crust. Then add:

2 packages instant pistachio pudding
2-1/2 cups milk

Mix and spread on cheese layer. Top with other half of Cool Whip® and sprinkle with chopped walnuts. Refrigerate.

Chocolate Chip Cheese Cake

1-1/2 cups Oreos®, finely crushed
2 to 3 tablespoons margarine, melted
3 8-ounce packages cream cheese, room temperature
1 14-ounce can Eagle® brand milk
3 eggs
2 teaspoons vanilla
1 cup miniature chocolate chips
1 teaspoon flour

Combine Oreo® crumbs and margarine, press firmly into 9 inch springform or 9 x 13 pan. Beat cream cheese until fluffy. Gradually beat in Eagle® brand till smooth. Add eggs and vanilla, mix well. In small bowl, toss 1/2 cup chips with flour to coat, stir in cheese mixture. Pour into pan, sprinkle remaining chips evenly over top. Bake at 300° for 55-60 minutes or till set. Cool. Chill any leftovers in the refrigerator.

Pineapple Ice Box Dessert

3/4 cup vanilla wafers, crushed
1/2 cup margarine, soft
1-1/2 cups powdered sugar
1 egg, beaten
1 cup heavy cream, whipped
1 can (1 pound 4 ounces) crushed pineapple
2/3 cup walnuts, coarsely chopped
Pineapple sauce

Day before: lightly grease 8 inch square pan. Press crumbs in bottom of pan. In medium bowl, cream margarine and sugar till fluffy. Add egg, beat well. Fold into whipped cream. Drain pineapple, reserve syrup for sauce. Fold in pineapple and nuts just till well combined. Put in pan evenly, sprinkle with rest of crumbs. Cover, refrigerate 24 hours. Top with Pineapple Sauce.

Pineapple Sauce:
1/2 cup sugar
1 tablespoon cornstarch
reserved syrup from pineapple
1/4 teaspoon grated lemon peel
1 8-ounce can crushed pineapple

Combine sugar and cornstarch in pan. Add water to syrup if necessary to make 3/4 cup stir till smooth. Add lemon peel and pineapple. Boil till thick and translucent. Cover and refrigerate.

Creamy Rice Pudding

1 cup rice
2 cups water
1 can evaporated milk
milk
1 cup sugar
1 teaspoon vanilla
2 tablespoons butter

Boil rice in water for 3 minutes, drain and add evaporated milk and enough milk to make 4 cups total. Cook slowly until thick and creamy. Add sugar, vanilla and butter. Mix well and cool. Great topped with strawberries.

Rosemary's Tapioca Pudding

This came from a lovely lady named Rosemary Rueden in Wisconsin.

1 box minute tapioca
1-1/3 cups sugar
3/4 teaspoon salt
12 cups milk
6 - 7 egg yolks
1 cup sugar
7 - 8 egg whites
4 teaspoons vanilla
1 small can crushed pineapple, drained

Bring the tapioca, 1-1/3 cups sugar, salt, milk and egg yolks to a full boil, stirring constantly. Beat the 1 cup sugar with the egg whites and gradually add the tapioca mixture. Add the vanilla. Cool slightly and add pineapple. You'll love this, and it can be halved.

Broiled Or Grilled Peaches

I've served these often with a heavy meal. They're light and very tasty.

medium to large peaches, halved and pitted
brown sugar
1 cup peach schnapps
1 tablespoon butter
1 tablespoon sugar
heavy cream
powdered sugar
cardamom
pecans

Sprinkle peaches with brown sugar and broil or grill until tender. In a small saucepan, mix the peach schnapps, butter and sugar. Simmer until reduced to a light syrup. Cool. Whip heavy cream with just a little powdered sugar. Add a dash or two of cardamom. Top warm peaches with cream, drizzle with peach syrup and sprinkle with chopped pecans. This is sooo good.

Chocolate Dessert

1 cup flour
1 cup sugar
2 teaspoons baking powder
1/4 teaspoon salt
1/2 cup milk
1 egg
1-1/2 squares chocolate, melted
1/2 cup brown sugar
1/2 cup granulated sugar
1 cup water
1 square chocolate, melted

Mix together the flour, sugar, baking powder and salt. Add milk, egg and 1-1/2 squares melted chocolate. Pour into greased pan. Mix the sugars, water and 1 square melted chocolate and pour on top. Bake at 350° for 30 minutes. Serve with whipped cream.

Taffy Apple Pizza
Julie gave me this… It's great!

1 package refrigerated peanut butter cookie dough (20 oz.)
3 tablespoons flour
1 8-ounce package cream cheese, softened
1/2 cup brown sugar, packed
1/2 teaspoon vanilla
2 medium baking apples (granny smith)
1 cup lemon lime soda
cinnamon
1/4 cup caramel topping
1/2 cup peanuts, chopped

Preheat oven to 350°. Remove 1/2 cup cookie dough for another use (otherwise the crust will be too thick). Add flour to remainder of dough and kneed. Press dough on baking stone. Stay 1 inch from the edge. Bake for 15-20 minutes or until lightly browned. Cool 10 minutes. Loosen cookie from baking stone and cool completely. Blend cream cheese, brown sugar and vanilla until smooth. Spread on crust. Dip sliced, peeled apples into soda to prevent browning. Drain and arrange on cream cheese mixture. Sprinkle with cinnamon and top with heated caramel sauce. Sprinkle peanuts on top.

Apple Dumplings

2 cups sugar
2 cups water
1/4 teaspoon cinnamon
1/4 teaspoon nutmeg
1/4 cup butter
6 apples, peeled and cut into 8ths

Make a syrup with the sugar, water, cinnamon and nutmeg, bring to a boil. Add butter, then set aside.

Crust:
2 cups flour
2 teaspoons baking powder
1 teaspoon salt
Cut in 3/4 cup margarine.
Add 1/2 cup milk all at once.
Stir to a ball.

On lightly floured board, roll dough to 1/4 inch thickness. Cut in 5 inch squares. Arrange 4 pieces of apple on each square. Sprinkle generously with cinnamon, sugar and nutmeg. Then dot with butter. Fold the corners of dough together, pinch the edges together and place dumpling into a greased baking pan, one inch apart. Cover with syrup. Bake at 375° for 30-40 minutes. Serve warm with cream or ice cream.

Gooey Butter Cake

1 package yellow cake mix (Duncan Hines® preferred)
1 stick margarine, melted
1 egg
1 8-ounce package cream cheese, softened
1 box powdered sugar
2 eggs
1 teaspoon vanilla

Grease 9 x 13 pan. Mix together the cake mix, margarine and egg. Press evenly into the greased pan. Combine the cream cheese, powdered sugar, eggs and vanilla. Spread evenly in pan over top of first mixture. Bake for 40 minutes at 350°. Sprinkle powdered sugar over top.

Apple Crisp

8 large tart apples, peeled, sliced
1 teaspoon cinnamon
3-1/8 cups brown sugar
1-1/4 cups quick oatmeal
1-3/4 cups flour
1/2 teaspoon salt
3/4 cup butter (cold)

Place sliced apples in greased 9 x 13 pan. Combine remaining ingredients together until crumbly. Spread evenly over apples and bake at 350° for about 45 minutes. You may have some topping left over, and it freezes well.

Rhubarb Crisp

6 cups rhubarb, diced
1-1/2 cups sugar mixed with 6 tablespoons flour
1-1/2 cups flour
1-1/2 cups brown sugar
1 cup oatmeal
1/2 cup margarine
1/2 cup shortening

In greased 9 x 13 pan put rhubarb, mixed with sugar. Then mix rest like pie crust and sprinkle over rhubarb. Bake at 375° for 40 minutes.

Lola's Rhubarb Dessert

1 yellow cake mix
4 cups rhubarb, diced
1 cup sugar
8 ounces whipping cream

Make the cake according to directions. Put into a 9 x 13 pan. Spread the rhubarb over the top of the batter. Dissolve the sugar in the whipping cream. Mix well, and drizzle over the rhubarb. Bake at 350° for about 35-40 minutes or until done. It's fun to layer some kind of berry with the rhubarb.

Desserts, Pies & Candies

Dream Rhubarb Dessert

2 cups flour
1/2 cup powdered sugar
1 cup margarine
2-1/2 cups sugar
1/2 cup flour
1-1/2 teaspoons salt
4 eggs, beaten
4 heaping cups rhubarb, sliced

For crust, mix 2 cups flour, powdered sugar and margarine like pie crust. Pat into 9 x 13 pan, bake 10 minutes at 350º. Mix sugar, 1/2 cup flour and salt, then add eggs and rhubarb. Pour over crust, bake 35 minutes at 350º.

Bananas Foster Dessert

1 pie crust, this can be homemade or from the dairy section in the market
2 teaspoons orange zest
4-1/2 teaspoons Rum or 4 teaspoons water and 1/2 teaspoon Rum flavoring
2 bananas, sliced about 1/4 inch
2/3 cup nuts (preferably pecans), chopped
2/3 cup brown sugar
1/4 cup heavy cream
1/4 cup butter
3/4 teaspoon vanilla

Bake the pie crust in a 9 inch pie tin or a removable bottom tart pan. Bake at 450º for 9-10 minutes. Cool. Spread the orange zest on the baked pie crust. Mix the rum and bananas together and layer evenly over the orange zest. Sprinkle nuts over the bananas. In a sauce pan bring the brown sugar, cream and butter to a boil, stirring constantly. Cook 2-4 minutes longer until it has gotten thick and is a golden brown color. Remove from the heat, add vanilla and pour carefully over the bananas. Cool and store in the refrigerator. Great with whipped cream or ice cream.

Pumpkin Praline Torte

This is just delicious!!

1/3 cup butter
3 tablespoons heavy cream
3/4 cup brown sugar
3/4 cup pecans, chopped

Cake:
4 eggs
1-2/3 cups sugar
1 cup oil
2 cups solid packed pumpkin
1/4 teaspoon vanilla
2 cups flour
2 teaspoons baking powder
2 teaspoons pumpkin pie spice
1 teaspoon baking soda
1 teaspoon salt

Topping:
1-3/4 cups whipping cream
1/4 cup powdered sugar
1/4 teaspoon vanilla
additional pecans

Combine butter, cream and brown sugar in a saucepan. Cook slowly until sugar dissolves. Pour into 2 - 9 inch greased cake pans and sprinkle nuts over the top. Cool.

To make the cake, beat together eggs, sugar and oil. Add pumpkin and vanilla. Combine dry ingredients and add to the pumpkin mixture. Mix until just blended and pour over the sugar and nuts in the cake pans. Bake at 350° for 30-35 minutes. Cool 5-10 minutes and remove from the pans. Cool completely on a rack. To assemble, place one cake, praline side up on plate. Beat whipping cream, sugar and vanilla until it forms soft peaks. Frost with 1/2 the cream, and top with remaining cake layer, praline side down. Top with the rest of the cream and sprinkle with pecans. Refrigerate.

Desserts, Pies & Candies

Pumpkin Roll

3 eggs, well beaten
1 cup sugar
2/3 cup solid packed pumpkin
1 teaspoon lemon juice
3/4 cup flour
1 teaspoon baking powder
1 teaspoon ginger
1/2 teaspoon nutmeg
2 teaspoons cinnamon
1 cup walnuts, chopped

Mix the eggs, sugar, pumpkin and lemon juice together well. Add the flour, baking powder, ginger, nutmeg and cinnamon. Line jelly role pan with wax paper. Spread batter in pan. Sprinkle chopped nuts over batter. Bake at 375° for 15 minutes. Turn cake onto damp dish towel, remove wax paper. Roll-up in towel and set for 1 hour.

Filling:
1 8-ounce package cream cheese
4 tablespoons butter
1 cup powdered sugar
1 teaspoon vanilla

Mix well. Spread on unrolled cake. Roll and sprinkle with powdered sugar. Chill. Freezes well, wrap in foil. Makes an excellent gift.

Meringues

6 egg whites
1/4 teaspoon cream of tartar
1-1/2 cups sugar

Beat egg whites and cream of tartar adding sugar slowly until stiff. About 20 minutes. Shape into small bowl (3 - 4 inches across), with a pastry bag or a spoon. Put into oven and bake for about an hour at 275°-300°. They are very crisp. Serve with a scoop of ice cream and top with berries or chocolate syrup.

Chocolate Eclair Cake

1 cup water
1/2 cup butter
1 cup flour
4 eggs

Filling:
2 3-ounce packages French vanilla pudding
2 cups milk
9 ounce container Cool Whip®
2 teaspoons vanilla

Bring the water and butter to a boil. Add flour and mix well, remove from heat. Add eggs, one at a time. Mix well after each addition (I do this step in my mixer). Put on ungreased pizza pan, and bake at 400° for 45-50 minutes. When cool, split in half and fill with the filling. To make filling combine the pudding and milk, add the Cool Whip® and vanilla. Replace top and drizzle chocolate glaze over top, recipe follows.

Chocolate Glaze
1 cup cream or half and half
2 cups of chocolate chips

Heat cream or half and half until hot, add chocolate chips, stirring until melted and combined over low heat.

Hot Fudge Sauce

1/2 cup margarine
3 squares unsweetened chocolate
2-1/2 cups sugar
1/2 teaspoon salt
1 large can evaporated milk
1 teaspoon vanilla

Melt margarine and chocolate in large pan, stirring. Add sugar gradually, 4 tablespoons at a time, stirring constantly. Add salt, then add the milk gradually. Add vanilla last. Cook until desired thickness, keeping in mind that this will thicken more when it is cool. Put into blender and blend for about a minute to smooth the sauce out. This can be stored for a long time in the refrigerator and reheated as needed. Makes about a quart.

Cream Puffs

1 cup water
1/2 cup butter, cut in pieces
1 cup flour
1/2 teaspoon salt
4 large eggs

Place water and butter in sauce pan. Bring to a full boil over medium heat. Boil until butter is melted. Add flour and salt, stir hard until dough forms a ball, about 1 minute. Remove from heat. Add eggs one at a time, mixing thoroughly after each one. Lightly grease a cookie sheet. Preheat oven to 400°. Using 1/4 cup drop mounds of dough about 3 inches apart on sheet. Bake 35-40 minutes until golden brown. Remove from oven, cool. Slit 1/3 off the top, remove any soft dough inside puffs. Spoon or pipe filling into puffs. Replace tops, sprinkle with powdered sugar. Serve immediately or refrigerate and serve within 2 hours. Makes 8-10 puffs.

Filling
1 box French vanilla pudding
2 cups milk
4 ounces cream cheese, softened
1 teaspoon vanilla
1 cup Cool Whip®

Prepare pudding according to directions, add remaining ingredients.

Cinnamon Sauce

3/4 cup sugar
1-1/2 cups apple juice
cornstarch to thicken
1 teaspoon cinnamon
1 teaspoon vanilla
1 tablespoon margarine

Bring sugar and apple juice to a boil, thicken with cornstarch and add rest of the ingredients. This is a great sauce over ice cream. Perhaps served in a crispy flour tortilla bowl dusted with cinnamon and sugar.

Eclairs

Prepare dough using cream puffs recipe on page 189. To form eclairs, use a pastry bag fitted with a 1/2 inch tip. Pipe dough into 4 x 1 inch fingers, leaving about 2 inches apart. Or spoon dough and shape with small spatula. Bake at 400° about 40 minutes or until golden. Remove from oven, cool. Prepare chocolate icing (recipe follows). Spoon filling into a pastry bag and fill or cut tops off each pastry and spoon filling into pastry. Replace tops and frost. Makes 10-12 eclairs.

Filling
1 box French vanilla pudding
2 cups milk
4 ounces cream cheese, softened
1 teaspoon vanilla
1 cup Cool Whip®

Prepare pudding according to directions, add remaining ingredients.

Chocolate Icing
2 squares semi-sweet chocolate or 1/3 cup chocolate chips
1 tablespoon butter
1/2 cup powdered sugar
1 to 2 tablespoons hot water

Melt chocolate and butter. Stir in rest until smooth. Add more hot water 1/2 teaspoon at a time until mixture drops off spoon in a thin ribbon.

Baked Cranberry Sauce

This recipe came from Vesta Fyvie, a good friend of my Mom's. She always made this during the holidays. It lasts a long time.

4 cups fresh cranberries
2 cups sugar
1/4 - 1/3 cup brandy

Clean and rinse cranberries. Place in a 9 x 13 inch pan and sprinkle with sugar. Cover pan with foil and bake for 1 hour at 300°. Stir gently every 20 minutes or so. Remove from the oven and add brandy. Stir gently. Cool and keep in the refrigerator.

Baklava

3 cups walnuts, finely chopped
1 teaspoon cinnamon, if desired
about 1 cup butter
1 pound fresh or frozen phyllo sheets
honey syrup, recipe follows

Combine walnuts and cinnamon. Set aside. Melt butter. Lightly brush a 9 x 13 pan with butter. Place 1 phyllo sheet in pan, folding to fit in pan. Lightly brush with butter. Repeat with 5 more phyllo sheets. Sprinkle the last sheet with a third of the nut mixture. Place 1 phyllo sheet on top of the nut layer, fitting pan. Lightly brush with butter. Repeat with 3 more phyllo sheets. Sprinkle the last sheet with half the remaining nut mixture. Place 1 phyllo sheet on top of nut layer folding to fit pan. Lightly brush with butter. Repeat with 3 more phyllo sheets. Sprinkle last sheet with rest of nut mixture. Top with remaining phyllo sheets, folding to fit pan and brushing each with butter. Press top layer firmly all over to lightly compact layers. Trim any pastry that sticks above top layer. Brush top with butter. (If needed, melt more butter.) Preheat oven to 350°. With the tip of a very sharp knife, score the top in diamond shapes. DO NOT CUT THROUGH LAYERS. Bake 30 minutes. Immediately after placing in oven, prepare honey syrup. After Baklava bakes 30 minutes, reduce heat to 300° and bake 30-40 minutes longer until light golden brown. Remove from oven, cut pastry on scored lines. Pour honey syrup evenly over cut pastry. Cool. Makes 40 servings.

Honey Syrup:
3/4 cup sugar
3/4 cup water
1 teaspoon lemon juice
1/3 cup honey

Combine sugar and water in saucepan. Stir often over medium heat until mixture comes to a full boil. Reduce heat and simmer 5 minutes. Stir in lemon and honey. Cool slightly.

A smile is a whisper of a laugh.

Caramel Fruit Dip

1 8-ounce container sour cream
1/2 teaspoon vanilla
1/2 jar caramel topping
1/2 cup brown sugar
1/2 cup walnuts

Put in blender, nuts go in last. Great dips for apples and other fruit.

Caramel Dip

THIS IS MY FAVORITE!!! It's Kathy Gustafson's recipe. She used to serve it to D.J.'s class at St. Francis on his birthday.

1 cup Karo® syrup
2 cups brown sugar
1/2 stick margarine
1 can sweetened condensed milk
dash of vanilla

Stir syrup, sugar and margarine until dissolved. Add sweetened condensed milk and vanilla. Great with apples, etc.

Liz's Fruit Dip

juice from 20-ounce can pineapple chunks
1 3-ounce French vanilla instant pudding (dry)
16 ounces sour cream

Mix juice and pudding, then fold in sour cream. This is a wonderful refreshing fruit dip and is especially good with strawberries.

Fruit Sauce

1 quart berries, reserving 1/3 to 1/2 of the berries
water
1/2 to 2/3 cup sugar
cornstarch

Cook berries down with a little water, reserving 1/3 to 1/2. Add sugar to taste. Thicken with a little cornstarch. Not too thick. After it's cooled slightly, add reserved berries. It's a great topping for cheese cake and also for the cream puff cake.

Desserts, Pies & Candies

No Fail Pie Crust

4 cups flour
1-3/4 cups margarine
1 tablespoon sugar
1 teaspoon salt
1 tablespoon vinegar
1 beaten egg
1/2 cup water

Mix first 4 ingredients. Add rest and mix well. Shape into a ball and chill at least 15 minutes before rolling. Roll on floured surface. Makes enough for 5 double crust pies. Can be frozen.

Graham Cracker Crust

1-1/4 cups graham cracker crumbs
1/3 cup melted butter or margarine
1/4 cup sugar

Combine all ingredients and press into 9 x 9 pan. Bake at 375° for 8 minutes. Cool before adding filling. Some pies call for an unbaked crust.

Meringue Topping for Pie

3 egg whites
1 tablespoon water
1/8 teaspoon salt
1/4 teaspoon cream of tartar
6 tablespoons sugar
3/4 teaspoon vanilla

Beat well until it holds it's shape, pile on pie and bake at 300° for 15-20 minutes.

Coconut Cream Pie

3/4 cup sugar
2 tablespoons flour
2 tablespoons cornstarch
1/4 teaspoon salt
2-1/2 cups milk
4 egg yolks
1 tablespoon butter
1 teaspoon vanilla
1 cup flake coconut
1 9 inch baked pie crust

In pan combine, sugar, flour, cornstarch and salt. In bowl, beat milk and yolks until smooth. Stir into sugar mixture, stirring constantly over medium heat until mixture thickens and comes to a boil. Stir and boil 1 minute. Remove from heat and stir in butter, vanilla and coconut. Pour into pie shell and top with meringue or with whipped cream. Sprinkle a little toasted coconut over the top.

Banana Cream Pie

Make coconut cream pie, but instead of adding coconut, slice 2 bananas into bottom of baked crust before adding filling. Top with meringue or whipped cream.

Blueberry Pie

1-1/2 to 1-3/4 cups sugar
3-1/2 - 4 tablespoons cornstarch or tapioca
1 tablespoon lemon juice
6 cups blueberries
9 inch double crust

Toss sugar, cornstarch and lemon juice with berries. Put into crust and cover with top crust. Brush with milk or water and sprinkle with sugar. Bake at 375° for 1 hour, until bubbly.

Desserts, Pies & Candies

Butterscotch Pie

This was a favorite of Grandma Hansen's and Gug's.

3/4 cup packed brown sugar
2 tablespoons flour
2 tablespoons butter
1/4 teaspoon salt
1 cup scalded milk
3 egg yolks
vanilla
1 baked pie crust

Combine the brown sugar, flour, butter and salt in a double boiler. Cook these ingredients until blended and add scalded milk. Beat the egg yolks until light. Pour a little of the milk mixture over the eggs. Beat a little with the eggs and return it all to the double boiler. Stir and cook until the mixture thickens. Cool and flavor with vanilla. Pour into a baked pie crust, top with meringue and bake at 300° for 15-20 minutes to lightly brown the meringue. I sometimes double the filling for a 9 or 10 inch pie crust, otherwise it's a little skimpy.

Best Apple Tart

This a wonderful alternative to an apple pie. It's easy and just as good.

1-1/4 cups flour
1/2 cup shortening
6 tablespoons water
5-6 baking apples
1/2 cup sugar
1/2 teaspoon cinnamon
1/4 teaspoon allspice
a pinch of ground cloves and nutmeg
1/4 cup butter
1/4 cup flour
1/3 cup sugar

Mix flour and shortening with hands until shortening is about pea size. Add water 1 tablespoon at a time. Roll and put into a flan or pie pan roughly. Cut and peel apples and mix with the sugar and spices, mixing well. Put in the center of the crust. Dot with butter and bring crust up around the apple mixture. Top with a mixture of the 1/4 cup butter, flour and sugar. Bake at 350° for about 1 hour.

Perfect Apple Pie

8 - 10 tart apples
3/4 - 1 cup sugar
2 tablespoons flour
1 teaspoon cinnamon
1/4 teaspoon nutmeg
dash of salt
pastry for a double crust pie
2 tablespoons margarine

Peel and slice apples. Combine sugar, flour, spices and salt. Mix with apples. Put into unbaked crust and dot with margarine. Cover with top crust. Brush with milk or water and sprinkle with sugar. Make small slashes in top. Bake at 375° for 40-50 minutes.

Fresh Berry Pie (Quick Berry Pie)

This recipe came from Lynne Giles at the Upper Crust. It's so good, that the last time my friend and I had it there we just got some forks and ate the rest right out of the pan. Mmmmmmmmmmm.

1 cup sugar
1 cup water
pinch of salt
3 tablespoons cornstarch
2 tablespoons corn syrup
3 tablespoons Jello®, flavor to compliment the berries used, i.e. lemon for
    blueberries, strawberry for strawberries
1 quart fresh berries

Cook the sugar, water, salt, cornstarch and corn syrup until thick and clear. Remove from heat and add Jello®. Line baked pie crust with berries. Pour mixture over berries and refrigerate until set.

Rhubarb Cream Pie

1-3/4 cups sugar
4 tablespoons flour
1/2 teaspoon nutmeg
4 eggs, beaten
2 teaspoons margarine
4 - 5 cups rhubarb, diced
pastry for a double crust pie

Blend sugar, flour, nutmeg and eggs, add margarine. Mix until smooth. Put rhubarb in unbaked pie shell and pour mixture over. Put on top crust and bake at 450° for 10 minutes, then at 350° for 30 minutes.

The difficulties in life are intended to make us better, not bitter.

Raisin Pie

2 cups raisins
1/2 cup sugar, mounded
water
1/4 cup milk or light cream
2 beaten eggs
3 level teaspoons cornstarch
1 teaspoon vanilla
1 baked pie crust

Cover raisins and sugar with water, 1 inch over raisins. Bring to a boil, simmer until softened. Mix until smooth, the milk or cream, eggs and cornstarch. Add vanilla. Mix with raisins and cook slowly until thick, stirring constantly. Pour into crust. Cool and serve with Cool Whip®.

Peach Pie

6 or more peaches, sliced
1 cup sugar
2 tablespoons flour
a pinch of cinnamon and nutmeg
a pinch of salt
2 tablespoons lemon juice
1/2 stick butter, melted
9 inch double crust

Mix all ingredients, except butter, with peaches. Put into prepared crust and drizzle the butter over the fruit. Cover with top crust, sprinkle with sugar and bake at 350° until bubbly, about 1 hour.

Lemon Meringue Pie

1-3/4 cups sugar
6 tablespoons cornstarch
2 tablespoons flour
1/2 teaspoon salt
4 egg yolks
1-3/4 cups water
1 tablespoon butter
1 tablespoon grated lemon peel
1/2 cup lemon juice
9 inch baked pie crust

In saucepan, combine sugar, cornstarch, flour and salt. In separate bowl beat egg yolks and water until smooth. Gradually stir into sugar mixture. Stir constantly over medium heat until mixture thickens and comes to a boil. Stir and boil 1 minute. Remove from heat, and stir in butter, lemon peel and lemon juice. Pour into crust and immediately top with meringue.

Pumpkin Pie

2 eggs
3/4 cup sugar
1 teaspoon cinnamon
1/2 teaspoon nutmeg
1/2 teaspoon salt
1/4 teaspoon ground cloves
1/4 teaspoon ginger
1 1-pound can pumpkin
1-2/3 cups evaporated milk

Combine all but pumpkin and milk. Mix well and add pumpkin. Gradually add milk and mix well. Pour into unbaked pie crust. Bake at 425° for 15 minutes, then at 350° for 40-45 minutes. Pie is done when knife inserted in center comes out clean.

Pumpkin Pie Option

1/2 cup brown sugar
1/3 cup chopped nuts
2 tablespoons butter

Mix and spread on unbaked crust. Bake at 350° for 10 minutes, then add pumpkin pie filling and bake according to the pumpkin pie directions.

German Sweet Chocolate Pie

1 package german sweet chocolate
1/3 cup milk
2 tablespoons sugar
1 8-ounce package cream cheese
8 ounces Cool Whip®
graham cracker crust

Heat chocolate and 2 tablespoons milk until melted. Beat sugar into cream cheese. Add remaining milk and chocolate mixture. Beat until smooth and fold in Cool Whip®. Combine well and put into crust. Freeze until firm.

Jello® Pecan Pie

1 small package vanilla pudding
1 cup corn syrup
3/4 cup evaporated milk
1 egg, lightly beaten
1 cup chopped pecans

Blend pudding mix with corn syrup. Gradually add milk and egg, stirring to blend. Add pecans and pour into an unbaked pie crust. Bake at 375° until top is firm and just begins to crack. About 40 minutes. Cool at least 3 hours.

Pecan Fudge Pie

4 ounces sweet cooking chocolate
1/4 cup margarine
1 can sweetened condensed milk
1/2 cup hot water
2 eggs, beaten
1 teaspoon vanilla
1/8 teaspoon salt
1-1/4 cups pecans, chopped or halved
9 inch unbaked crust

Melt chocolate and margarine. Stir in milk, water and eggs. Mix well. Remove from heat and stir in remaining ingredients. Pour into crust and bake at 350° for 40-45 minutes or until center is set. Cool.

Nut Clusters

12 ounces chocolate chips
1/2 cup peanut butter, smooth or chunky
2 cups dry roasted peanuts, coarsely chopped

Melt chips and peanut butter, stir in peanuts. Drop by teaspoonful into foil cupcake papers (mini) or onto waxed paper. Chill and store in refrigerator. This can also be done with raisins.

Desserts, Pies & Candies

Gug's Nut Brittle

1 cup brown sugar
1 cup butter
pinch of cream of tartar
7 Hershey® bars
nuts, finely chopped

Over low heat, in a heavy pan, cook brown sugar, butter and cream of tartar. Heat to hard crack stage. Spoon onto greased drip pan, cover with chocolate and spread evenly. Sprinkle with nuts. Let stand overnight, then break.

Peanut Brittle

2 cups sugar
1 cup corn syrup
1/2 cup water
1/4 teaspoon salt
2 cups peanuts
2 teaspoons baking soda

Boil sugar, corn syrup, water and salt to 265 degrees on a candy thermometer. Add peanuts and boil to 310 degrees. Add baking soda. Spread on greased jelly roll pan and any left over on a plate. Crack when it's hard.

Texas Millionaires

1 package caramels
2 tablespoons evaporated milk
2 cups walnuts, chopped
6 Hershey® bars, melted

Grease wax paper well. Melt caramels and milk. Stir in walnuts, drop by teaspoonfuls onto wax paper. Frost each with melted chocolate. Cool.

Five Minute Fudge

4 tablespoons margarine
2/3 cup evaporated milk
3 cups sugar
1/2 teaspoon salt
1 7-ounce jar marshmallow cream
12 ounces chocolate chips
1 teaspoon vanilla
1 cup walnuts, chopped

Bring to a boil margarine, milk, sugar and salt over medium heat. Boil 5 minutes stirring constantly. Remove from heat and stir in marshmallow cream, chips, vanilla and walnuts. Pour into well buttered 9 x 13 pan. Cool and cut into squares.

Buckeyes

A wonderful little peanut butter candy.

1/2 pound margarine
1-1/2 pounds powdered sugar
1 pound peanut butter
12 ounces chocolate chips
6 ounces butterscotch chips
1/8 block of paraffin

Mix together the margarine, powdered sugar and peanut butter and roll into balls. About 1 inch. Dip into a mixture of chocolate chips, butterscotch chips, and paraffin melted together. Leave just a small spot of the peanut butter ball uncoated. Thus the name—Buckeyes.

Chocolate Cream Balls

1/2 pound melting chocolate
1/2 cup whipping cream
walnuts, chopped

Melt chocolate and cool. Whip cream and fold into chocolate. Chill until firm. Form into balls and roll in walnuts.

Desserts, Pies & Candies

New York Squares

This is a very good candy bar. It's Guggie's recipe.

First layer:
2 squares semi-sweet chocolate
1 stick margarine
1 egg, beaten
1 teaspoon vanilla
2 cups graham cracker crumbs
1 cup flake coconut
1/2 cup nuts

Melt chocolate with margarine. Add egg and vanilla, mix and add graham cracker crumbs, coconut and nuts. Press into 10 inch pan, chill.

Second layer:
1/2 stick margarine
2 cups powdered sugar
2 tablespoons instant vanilla pudding
3 tablespoons milk
3 drops green food coloring
1/2 teaspoon vanilla
1/4 teaspoon peppermint

Melt margarine, add powdered sugar, vanilla pudding, milk, food coloring, vanilla and peppermint. Blend well, spread on first layer.

Third layer:
3 squares semi-sweet chocolate
1-1/2 teaspoons margarine

Melt chocolate and margarine. Spread over second layer and refrigerate. Cut into small squares and serve.

If you want to avoid being tempted to eat forbidden fruit,
stay out of the devil's kitchen.

Christmas Balls

12 ounces chocolate chips
1 can sweetened condensed milk
1 cup nuts, chopped
1 teaspoon vanilla
1-1/2 cups coconut
Chopped nuts

Melt chips over medium heat. Remove and add milk, nuts and vanilla. Cool. Roll into balls and roll in coconut and/or chopped nuts.

Pralines

The best!!! You'll think you're on Bourbon Street in New Orleans.

2 cups granulated sugar
1 cup half and half
3 tablespoons butter
1/8 teaspoon baking soda
1-3/4 cup nuts (pecans are best)

Bring to a boil the first four ingredients, cook to softball stage (about 240°), stirring constantly. Remove from heat, add nuts and beat till it becomes opaque. Drop on sprayed wax paper. Try not to eat them all at once.

Caramels

1 cup butter
2-1/4 cups firmly packed brown sugar
1/8 teaspoon salt
1 cup light corn syrup
14 ounces sweetened condensed milk
1 teaspoon vanilla

In sauce pan, melt butter, stir in sugar and salt, then add corn syrup and mix well. Add milk, stirring constantly. Continue stirring and cook to 245 degrees. Remove from heat and stir in vanilla. Pour into 9 inch buttered pan or fill candy mold covered with chocolate.

Peanut Butter Fudge

This is Mildred's recipe and it's great.

2 cups sugar
2 cups brown sugar
1 cup evaporated milk
2 tablespoons butter
1-1/2 cups peanut butter
1 jar marshmallow cream
2 teaspoons vanilla
nuts

Cook the sugars, evaporated milk and butter to soft ball stage, then add the peanut butter, marshmallow cream and vanilla. Beat until set. Will be soft, but not runny. Add nuts and put into 9 x 13 pan and set.

Divinity

2-2/3 cups sugar
2/3 cup corn syrup
1/2 cup water
2 egg whites
1 teaspoon vanilla
2/3 cup walnuts, chopped

Stir sugar, syrup and water over low heat. Bring to 260 degrees. DO NOT STIR! Beat the egg whites until stiff and keep beating while pouring the hot mixture in a thin stream. Then add vanilla and walnuts. Beat until it holds it's shape and is slightly dull. Drop on waxed paper.

Hard Candy

powdered sugar
1-1/2 cups corn syrup
1 cup water
3-3/4 cups sugar
flavorings and colors, if desired

Sprinkle cookie sheet with plenty of powdered sugar. In pan, bring syrup, water and sugar to 310 degrees. DO NOT STIR! Take off heat immediately and add as much flavoring and coloring as you want. Pour into strips on cookie sheet, and cool. Break into pieces.

Caramel Corn

This stuff is addicting!!

1/2 pound butter (not margarine)
1 cup brown sugar
1/2 cup corn syrup
1 teaspoon baking soda
1 8-ounce bag hulless popcorn (puff corn)

To make the caramel sauce combine in a 2 quart saucepan, the butter, sugar and corn syrup, cook for 2 minutes. Add the baking soda to mixture, this will cause it to foam. Pour mixture over corn puffs and stir until mixed. Place in 250 degree oven for 45 minutes. Stir at least every 10-15 minutes. Remove from oven and pour on waxed paper and break apart.

Pickles, Marinades, Mixes, Etc.

Pickles, Marinades, Mixes, Etc.

Ettie's Pickles

This is Cindy Webb's Aunt Ettie's recipe. Cindy was our neighbor in Neenah and I've used it since we lived there.

cucumbers, small
garlic cloves
cream of tartar

Pack sterile jars with cucumbers, the smaller the better. Put 1 clove of garlic on the top and bottom of each jar. Put 1 teaspoon of cream of tartar in each quart. Cover with this brine.

1 cup salt
4 cups cider vinegar
12 cups water
1/2 cup sugar

Bring just to a boil. Pour over cucumbers and seal jars. In canning kettle, hot water bathe just until cucumbers change color a little.

Refrigerator Pickles

This is a very quick, very good and long lasting pickle.

6 cups cucumber, thinly sliced
1 cup onion, thinly sliced
1 cup bell pepper, thinly sliced
1 tablespoon salt
1 teaspoon celery seed, mustard seed or both
2 cups sugar
1 cup vinegar (cider)

Mix cucumbers, onions and peppers. Sprinkle with salt and refrigerate 2 hours. Remove and drain. Heat spices, sugar and vinegar until sugar dissolves. Pour over drained pickle mixture, and store in covered container in refrigerator.

Sweet Pickles (9 day crock pickles)

Put water in crock with enough salt to float an egg. Put whole pickles in crock for 3 days. Throw water away and rinse pickles well. Put fresh water on pickles. Change water every day for 3 days. Cut pickles into chunks before putting in vinegar. Combine and bring to simmer, 2/3 cup vinegar and 1/3 cup water and 1 tablespoon alum for each quart of pickles. Put pickles in brine and simmer until color turns. Let stand in brine 12 hours to 3 days. Throw old brine away and make sharp brine. 1 pint vinegar, 6 cups sugar, cloves and 1 cinnamon stick. Heat and pour over pickles. Let stand 3 days. Reheat to boiling and seal in jars.

Beet Pickles

3 pounds beets
1 stick cinnamon
1 teaspoon whole allspice
6 whole cloves
1 pint vinegar
1/2 cup sugar
1/2 cup water

Cook beets until tender. Remove skins, roots and tops. Tie spices in bag. Heat vinegar, sugar, water and spices to boiling. Add beets, whole, sliced or quartered. Boil for 5 minutes. Pack in sterile jars, fill with brine and seal. Makes 3 pints.

Make Your Own Vanilla

1 vanilla bean
1 cup vodka

Split vanilla bean down the center and cut it into small pieces. Put this into a glass jar containing vodka. Cover tightly, shake well and refrigerate. Shake the jar daily and don't use for 3 weeks. Makes realllllly good vanilla.

Pickles, Marinades, Mixes, Etc.

Barbecue Sauce

2-1/2 cups catsup
1/2 cup brown sugar
1/2 cup cider vinegar
1 tablespoon horseradish
1 tablespoon Worcestershire sauce
1 teaspoon garlic salt

Mix well and use as is. Keep in refrigerator. Best Sauce!!

Teriyaki Sauce

1/4 cup soy sauce
1/8 teaspoon garlic powder
1/2 teaspoon ginger
1/2 teaspoon pepper
1 tablespoon onion, chopped
1 tablespoon brown sugar
1 tablespoon oil
2 teaspoons water
2 tablespoons wine (optional)

Mix well. This is a wonderful marinade and basting sauce for meat and poultry.

Teriyaki Meat Marinade

1/2 cup soy sauce
1/2 cup dry sherry
1/4 cup white vinegar
1/4 cup water
1/2 teaspoon ginger
1/8 teaspoon garlic powder

Use this as a marinade for pork, beef and lamb.

Easy Meat Marinade

1 8-ounce bottle of red wine vinegar salad dressing
1/4 cup apple juice
2 teaspoons oregano
2 teaspoons basil
2 teaspoons prepared horseradish

This is another good marinade for pork, beef and lamb.

Tangy Meat Marinade

2/3 cup oil
1/4 cup steak sauce
1/4 cup dry sherry
1/4 cup red wine vinegar
1 tablespoon Worcestershire sauce

Keep this and the other marinades in a screw top jar. Marinate and baste with it.

Hot Chocolate Mix

12-14 quarts of nonfat dried milk
32 ounces Nestle's Quick®
2 pounds powdered sugar
1 large jar creamer

Mix together. Fill cup with 1/3 cup mix and fill with water. This makes a lot and lasts a long time. Easy for the kids to use.

Salt Substitute

1 teaspoon chili powder
1 tablespoon garlic powder
2 tablespoons dry mustard
6 tablespoons onion powder
2 teaspoons oregano
3 tablespoons paprika
2 teaspoons pepper
1 tablespoon poultry seasoning

Pickles, Marinades, Mixes, Etc.

Onion Soup Mix

2 cups instant minced onion
1/4 cup onion powder
1 cup instant beef bouillon
1 tablespoon beau monde

Store in tightly covered jar. A quarter cup of this mix is equal to 1 envelope of onion soup mix.

Seasoned Salt

1 box un-iodized salt
1-1/2 ounces black pepper
2 ounces red pepper
1 ounce garlic powder or salt
1 ounce chili powder
1 ounce accent

Mix and store in airtight quart jar.

People who try to do something and fail are much better off than those who try nothing.

Master Mix

10-1/2 cups all-purpose flour
1/4 cup plus 1 teaspoon baking powder
1 tablespoon plus 1-1/2 teaspoons salt
2 cups shortening

Mix flour, baking powder, and salt in a 4 quart bowl. Cut in shortening until mixture resembles fine crumbs. Cover, label and store in airtight container at room temperature for no longer than 3 months. Use for biscuits, pancakes, waffles or whatever.

Sweetened Condensed Milk

1 cup instant nonfat milk
1/3 cup boiling water
2/3 cup sugar
3 tablespoons butter, melted

Process all ingredients in blender and store in refrigerator. Makes 1 cup.

Homemade Dog Food

Don't we just love our Pups? I have 2 mini doxies and my little female (Callie) has a very delicate system, so I decided to cook for them. It's good for them, they love it and I love that it costs less than good canned food with very little effort. This is the stew that I make them.

1 pound very lean ground beef or any other lean meat, browned
1 pound poached chicken (preferably dark meat), shredded or diced
2 cups brown rice, cooked or diced or shredded hash browns
1 cup chicken broth, no salt
pinch of granulated garlic
2 cups frozen or canned vegetables, no salt

To the cooked meat, add brown rice or hash browns. Sometimes I add 1/2 cup quick oatmeal (dry) to the meat instead. Whatever you use, add chicken broth and garlic. If you use oatmeal, use 1-1/4 cups broth. When this is well mixed, add vegetables. Do not use corn or carrots. Beans or broccoli are good. Mine love Brussels sprouts. I get 6 days supply from this. Depends on the size of your baby. They'll smile and so will you. I'm working on some kitty things, but that's for another day, another book.

Index

Index